simply
south africa

a culinary journey

text by elaine hurford

food photography by craig fraser
and ryno

simply
south africa

a culinary journey

Struik Publishers (Pty) Ltd
(a member of Struik New Holland Publishing (Pty) Ltd)
Cornelis Struik House
80 McKenzie Street
Cape Town 8001

Reg. No.: 54/00965/07

ISBN 1 86872 436 0

First published in 2000
10 9 8 7 6 5 4 3 2 1

designer: Petal Palmer
design assistant: Illana Fridkin
editor: Elizé Lübbe
publishing manager: Linda de Villiers
picture researcher: Colette Stott
stylists: Sylvie Hurford and Justine Kiggen
food stylists' assistants: Andrea Steer and Elizabeth Copeland
photographers: Craig Fraser and Ryno
map: Steven Felmore

reproduction by Hirt & Carter
printed and bound by Tien Wah Press Pte Ltd, Singapore

Photographic credits

CPL = Cape Photo Library   SIL = Struik Image Library
NDWP = Nigel Dennis Wildlife Photography

Pages 2 Mike Allwood-Coppin/NDWP; 6 Walter Knirr; 7 Roger de la
Harpe/AFRICA IMAGERY; 8 (top) Shaen Adey; 8 (bottom) Erhardt
Thiel/SIL; 10 (left) Annelene Oberholzer; 10 (right) Nigel J Dennis;
11 (left) Roger de la Harpe/AFRICA IMAGERY; 11 (right) Walter Knirr/SIL;
12 Annelene Oberholzer; 13 (top) Erhardt Thiel/SIL; 14 (top) Shaen
Adey;15 (top) Shaen Adey; 15 (bottom) Jèan du Plessis; 16 (top) Shaen
Adey; 16 (bottom) Alain Proust; 17 (top) Alain Proust; 18–27 Ryno/SIL;
28 (left) Walter Knirr; 28 (right) Alain Proust; 29 (left) Walter Knirr;
29 (right) Mark Skinner; 30 Nigel J Dennis; 31 Chad Henning/CPL;
32 Walter Knirr; 33 Alain Proust; 34–35 Mark Skinner; 36 (top) Lanz von
Hörsten; 36 (bottom) Mike Allwood-Coppin/NDWP; 37 (top) Lanz von
Hörsten; 38–49 Craig Fraser/SIL; 50 (left) Hein von Hörsten/SIL;
50 (right) Walter Knirr; 51 (left and right) Nigel J Dennis;
52 and 53 Annelene Oberholzer; 54 Nigel J Dennis; 55 Keith Young/SIL;
56–65 Ryno/SIL; 66 (left and right) Walter Knirr; 67 (left) Nigel J Dennis;
67 (right) Roger de la Harpe/AFRICA IMAGERY; 68–71 Walter Knirr;
72 (top) Jèan du Plessis; 72 (bottom) Alain Proust; 74–83 Craig Fraser/SIL;
84 (left) Shaen Adey; 84 (right) Keith Young/CPL; 85 (left) Keith Young/SIL;
85 (right) Walter Knirr; 86 and 87 Shaen Adey; 88 and 89 Nigel J Dennis;
90 Edward Ruiz/iAfrika Photos; 91 and 92 Roger de la Harpe/AFRICA
IMAGERY; 93 Nigel J Dennis; 94–103 Ryno/SIL; 104 (left) Walter Knirr;
104 (right) Eric Miller/iAfrika Photos; 105–107 Walter Knirr; 108 Nigel J
Dennis; 109 Walter Knirr; 110–117 Craig Fraser/SIL; 118 (left and right)
Walter Knirr; 119 (left) Walter Knirr/SIL; 119 (right) Walter Knirr;
120–121 Walter Knirr; 122/123 Athol Franz; 124 and 125 Walter Knirr;
126 (bottom) Athol Franz/Gallo Images; 127 (top) Walter Knirr;
128–137 Ryno/SIL. 138 (left) Nigel J Dennis; 138 (right) Roger de la
Harpe/AFRICA IMAGERY; 139 (left and right) Nigel J Dennis; 140 Walter
Knirr; 141 Roger de la Harpe/AFRICA IMAGERY; 142 Walter Knirr;
143 Shaen Adey; 144 and 145 Nigel J Dennis; 146–153 Craig Fraser/SIL.

Photographers' acknowledgements
The publisher and photographers would like to thank Hotchi
Witchi, Lim, The Banks Shop, The Bright House, Peter Visser,
Yellow Door and Loft Living for the generous loan of the props
used in the food photographs.

contents

A journey through South Africa is destined to be sheer adventure for the senses. No matter how long the road or where it leads, the traveller will be lavishly assaulted by the sights and sounds, tastes and smells, colours and textures, of one of the most varied and beautiful countries in the world.

Its cities are sophisticated first-world metropoli, while the third world takes hold in sparsely populated rural areas where people live in traditional villages or in sprawling shanty towns on the fringes of the cities. Wherever the visitor finds himself he can be assured of a warm welcome. The country is renowned for its hospitality, which however humble, inevitably includes offers of food, drink and often, shelter.

It is a country with wonderful natural resources – fishing and agriculture are among the highest-ranking earners – producing almost all its own staples, as well as tea and nuts, tropical and deciduous fruits, vegetables, meat, fish and game, ostrich and for the adventurous, crocodile, mopane worms and wild greens such as indigenous spinach and cabbage.

South African cuisine is today, broadly, a hybrid of European, Asian and African influences. It is no problem to find eating places and community enclaves that have retained or in some cases, revived the country's colourful culinary traditions in their purest ethnic form: African, English, French, German, Dutch, Chinese, Indian, Greek, Portuguese – every city has these and more. But it is the fusion of east and west, old and new, and the introduction of a distinctive and updated African flavour that makes for an exciting culinary journey.

Tracing the origins of the South African table, one must begin with the San people who gathered the fruits of the sea and the veld. With the arrival of the Dutch in 1652, and later, slaves and political exiles from Indonesia, the menu expanded and was made exotic with spices from the east. Blending these early ingredients into what may diffidently be called

Above: *Durban's Sunday market is ablaze with fresh flowers.*
Opposite: *South Africa is world famous for its beautiful beaches.*

cuisine, was almost entirely attributable to the women who, in far-off lands, like their pioneering sisters the world over, became adept at improvising for the home and the table. From the handful of writers who have recorded the country's culinary history, we learn that food was gleaned from land and sea, river and veld. According to C Louis Leipoldt, renowned writer and legendary cook, the first Dutch settlers, sent to establish a refreshment station at the Cape, ate penguins, salted and stored in barrels. Tortoise and porcupine, locusts and leguaans, seals and even rock rabbits, found their way to the table.

Francois le Vaillant (the 18th century naturalist/explorer) breakfasted off the barbecued foot of a hippopotamus and enjoyed the trunk of a freshly shot elephant, dressed and roasted on an open fire, followed by the foot, next day, for breakfast.

'Never can our modern epicures have such a dainty at their tables. I thought it delicious,' he pronounced.

The corned tongues of eland were such a delicacy that the beast was extinct in the Cape by 1836. Another animal snuffed out for food was the quagga, fed by farmers to their servants. Pot roasted with bacon, herbs and brandy, the kori bustard was so highly regarded that it would have been eradicated by now if it had not been protected.

In times of plenty, the pioneer women preserved and pickled the remains of the hunt and the season's fruit and vegetables for leaner days. Onions, potatoes and pumpkins were stored in lofts and larders, together with dried meat (biltong) and fruit. This waste-not-want-not philosophy was born not only of piety but necessity, in a country where the climate was harsh and the future uncertain. From it evolved enduring delicacies such as 'kerriebone' (curried green beans), 'slaphakskeentjies' (onions in a creamy sauce of cooked vinegar, egg, mustard and sugar) and 'smoorsnoek' (air dried or smoked snoek braised with potatoes).

No part of the animal went to waste: sheep's liver was wrapped in caul fat, pigs' intestines were used as casings for rich pork and venison sausage spiked with coriander and lemon zest, and sheeps' heads and trotters were stewed or converted to brawn and stored in a cool room to keep them fresh.

In its early form, South African cuisine – much like that of provincial France and Italy – centred around luxuriously unhurried cooking, which released full, rich flavours. Roasts of mutton and venison were heavy with the smoke of the wood-burning stoves, the bread crusty from hours in a slow-cooling clay oven. Cape Dutch cuisine favoured the 'meat with sweet' combination, introduced by the Malay people, and echoing the British custom of serving fruit jellies or sauces with pork and game. Sweet potatoes served with

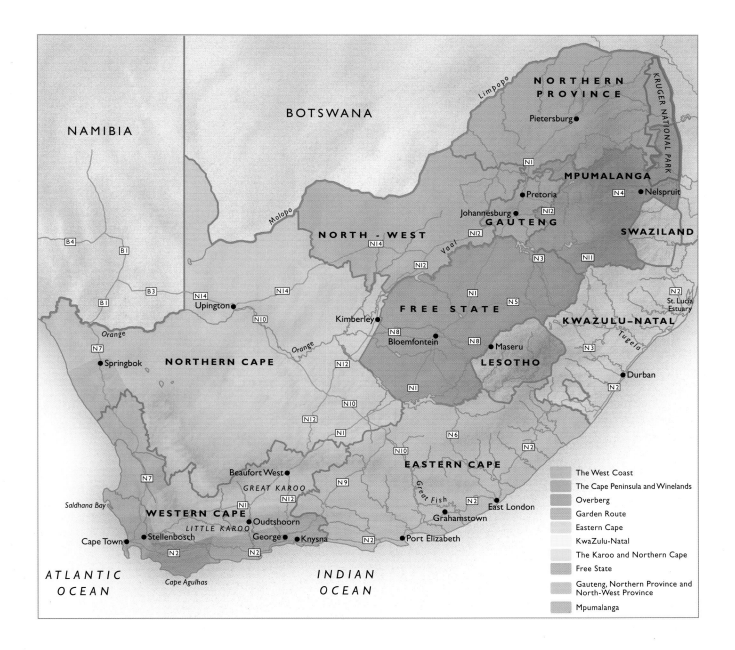

the meal were sticky with brown sugar, and spiced with cinnamon and dried naartjie peel; preserves of quince and apricot in clear, jewel-coloured sauces accompanied the meats. Beetroot and pumpkin were prepared in 101 ways, and the fruit of the fast-growing watermelon was converted into a preserve, which, presented with cheese at the end of a meal, provided a celestial dessert.

It was only with the arrival of the Huguenots in 1688 that the wine acquired real finesse, and it was they who introduced the beautiful preserves and confits to our cuisine.

Today urban chefs are looking back at the basics and taking them into the future with innovative adaptations, helping to evolve a truly distinctive style that can take its place with pride among the regional cuisines of the world.

fishing boat

seashells

the west coast

fishermen   paternoster

The Western seaboard of South Africa is one of the country's most intriguing destinations, an hour by road but worlds apart from Cape Town.

As the city recedes along the westbound marine boulevard, panoramic vistas encompass lagoons and wetlands, beautiful, if windswept beaches, the eastern face of the World Heritage Site Robben Island, and a breathtaking view of Table Mountain across the blue waters of Table Bay.

Above: *Bunches of bokkoms (herring) and harders, salted and air dried, are a favourite local snack.*

This is just the beginning of a road that will ultimately deposit the traveller far to the north on the rugged western shores of a fascinating coastal desert. On the way, and if the season is right, he will find dazzling displays of wild flowers, and feast on fresh-caught rock lobster or snoek (cod) straight off the boats. He will rub shoulders with rough, hospitable fisherman and perhaps even be offered a diamond from the alluvial diggings in the north.

He will journey through tiny villages with whitewashed houses hunched under thatch and small harbours with bright boats labouring under the day's haul. There will be salted fish strung up to dry and simple restaurants serving robust fare; this is centred around the abundant harvests of the sea and served with regional wines that are appropriately light and friendly.

Some of the eateries are no more than a rough shelter at the water's edge, but even dyed-in-the-wool Capetonians leave home for the crusty bread and jam, bubbling seafood broths, grilled shellfish and other ocean produce prepared simply and eaten al fresco.

Opposite: *Fishing trawlers lie at anchor in the quiet predawn at Lambert's Bay harbour. The day's haul will deliver rock lobster or snoek, calamari and linefish, depending on the season.*

The 300-kilometre coastal stretch from Yzerfontein in the south to Doringbaai in the north, is lobster territory, home of *Jasus lalandii*. But demand has grown so much for this delectable ocean scavenger that supplies are sometimes scarce. The West Coast seas are South Africa's most important commercial fishing grounds, with the celebrated rock lobster the prized catch. The abundant snoek is the real dietary staple on this coast. It is smoked, or barbecued under a coating of apricot jam, lemon juice and oil, which gives an excellent colour and complements the firm, salty flesh.

*Above: A vast colony of Cape gannets (*Morus capensis*) is one of 150 species on Bird Island, Lambert's Bay. Visitors can view the birds from an elevated observation platform at the end of a walkway connecting the 'island' with the harbour.*

Opposite top: Striking rock formations in the Cederberg Wilderness Area, where many San rock art sites are preserved.

*Opposite bottom: The Richtersveld National Park occupies 160 000 hectares of stark landscape on the southern banks of the Orange River. The quiver tree (*Aloe dichotoma*), foreground, is also known as the 'kokerboom'.*

Inland, farmers grow superb potatoes, which are an essential ingredient in 'smoorsnoek' – a truly South African dish combining snoek, potatoes and onions in a delicious kedgeree eaten with home-baked bread and 'korrelkonfyt' (whole grape jam). Conditions along the West Coast are also ideal for black mussels, and mussel 'farming' has become a very profitable business.

In spite of good food and wine, and plenty of it, the West Coast is a hard place to live. The climate is unforgiving, scoured by winds off the cold Atlantic Ocean, wilting under the summer heat. The landscape is lightly clad with sparse but hardy vegetation and frequently draped with damp sea mists. These mists are life giving to a fascinating variety of plants that erupt in a blaze of flowers in early spring, after rain. Festivals bring tiny towns to life, and busloads of sightseers come to witness the floral phenomenon, which peaks in August and September.

Like its specialised plants, the people of the West Coast are an adaptable lot – hard-working communities with simple needs bound by the daily demands of survival. They have lived and worked for generations in simple, workmanlike settlements, which have become hideaways for a special kind of tourist, spellbound by the stark beauty of the region and revering its simplicity and integrity.

The lagoon at Langebaan is the centrepiece of the West Coast National Park, a rigorously protected wetland area incorporating one of the world's top four bird sanctuaries. In summer, visitors will include 35 000 curlew sandpipers who have left their Arctic habitat for a season in the sun – just one small community of a rich population of avian fauna that brings artists, photographers and naturalists from all over the world. This area has protected itself with a series of almost contiguous reserves, ensuring that its simplicity and serenity will remain intact.

Below: *A shallow lagoon sprawls across one-third of the important West Coast National Park, which provides an unusually rich food source – including 550 species of invertebrates – for the myriad birds that find shelter here.*

Right: *Namaqualand erupts in a blaze of wild flowers after rain, bringing coachloads of visitors to the region in early spring, August and September each year.*

Left: *Spring flowers make an informal garden for a farmhouse on the outskirts of the tiny West Coast town of Nieuwoudtville. The mixed colours are an indication of well-balanced soil, while spreads of single colours are said to indicate soil that has been depleted.*

deep-fried calamari rings

Vissermans Kombuis, Paternoster, West Coast

125 g cleaned calamari
   rings
cake flour
cajun seasoning
salt and pepper
oil for deep frying

to serve
tartare sauce

Place flour and seasoning in a container. Add calamari and shake container to cover rings with flour mixture. Deep fry in oil for 45 seconds at 180 °C. Serve on rice or with chips, with tartare sauce on the side.

serves 1

wine suggestion
Weskus Blanc de Blanc

mussel and bacon bites

Slipway Waterfront Restaurant, Saldanha Bay

15 fresh West Coast
   mussels
1 onion, sliced
15 rashers rindless
   streaky bacon
125 ml cake flour
2 eggs, beaten
125 ml breadcrumbs
oil for deep frying
fresh lemon slices and
   salad greens for garnish
tartare sauce

Scrub mussels. Place in a heavy-bottomed pot with a tight-fitting lid, together with the sliced onion and a little water, and steam on high heat until the shells open. Discard any mussels that remain closed. Discard onion. Remove mussels from shells. Wrap each mussel in a strip of bacon and secure with a toothpick. Dip into flour, then egg, then roll in breadcrumbs to coat evenly. Deep-fry in hot oil until golden brown. Remove, drain and serve immediately on a plate garnished with salad greens, lemon slices and tartare sauce.

serves 3

wine suggestion
Theunisklraal Riesling

mussel and bacon bites   deep-fried calamari rings

fresh mussels in an onion
cream sauce

pickled mussels

fresh mussels in an onion cream sauce

The Old Palm Restaurant, St Helena Bay

Scrub the mussels and remove the beards. Chop the onions, garlic, green pepper and celery leaves. Heat a heavy-bottomed pot, add water, mussels and vegetables. Cover and bring to a boil. The mussels will begin to open after about 5 minutes. Shake the pot once or twice to distribute heat evenly. Do not overcook. Remove from heat. Discard shells as well as any unopened mussels.

For the sauce, soften onions in olive oil in a deep, heavy-bottomed pan until translucent and coated with oil. Add white wine and raise the heat to reduce the liquid by about half. Add mussels and stir occasionally, spooning the juices over the mussels. Add cream and a few turns of freshly ground black pepper, and stir. Serve straight from the pan, with a fresh baguette to mop up the juices.

serves 4

wine suggestion
Swartland Blanc de Blanc

32 mussels
1 onion
2 cloves garlic
1 large green pepper
1 bunch celery leaves
250 ml water

sauce
2 onions, finely chopped
45 ml olive oil
500 ml white wine
250 ml single cream
freshly ground black
  pepper

pickled mussels

The Old Palm Restaurant, St Helena Bay

Prepare the mussels as above. Remove the mussels from the shells and strain the juices from the pot into a bowl – there should be about 250 ml of juices.

Place the mussels in a sterilised glass jar along with one red or green chilli, black peppercorns, cloves and bay leaf. Cover with reserved mussel juices and white spirit vinegar. Top up with olive oil. Screw the lid on tightly and place in the refrigerator. The mussels can be eaten the following day and will last up to six weeks in the refrigerator. Serve on savoury biscuits or use in a seafood salad.

serves 4

wine suggestion
Swartland Blanc de Blanc

32 mussels
1 onion
2 cloves garlic
1 large green pepper
1 bunch celery leaves
250 ml water

pickling mixture
1 small red or green chilli
5 ml whole black
  peppercorns
5 whole cloves
1 bayleaf
125 ml spirit vinegar
30 ml olive oil

neptune's choice

Slipway Waterfront
Restaurant,
Saldanha Bay

In a bowl, combine the stock, lemon juice, honey, sherry, ginger, soya sauce, onion and lemon rind. Pour mixture into a large, deep pan with a lid (the pan must be wide enough to hold all the fish in a single layer). Heat slowly until the sauce starts to bubble, then cook for 5 minutes to give the various flavours time to develop. Add the fish, cover and simmer until the fish is cooked. Remove the fish and keep warm. Remove lemon rind from the sauce. Mix the butter and flour to a paste, then stir into the sauce a teasoonful at a time. Simmer until the sauce thickens.

To serve, pour sauce over fish. Sprinkle roasted sesame seeds and chopped parsley over the fish and serve immediately on a bed of rice.

serves 4

wine suggestion
Simonsig Chardonnay

4 x 200 g-portions kingklip
500 ml fish or chicken
   stock
50 ml lemon juice
20 ml honey
60 ml medium-dry sherry
5 ml grated fresh ginger
30 ml soya sauce
4 onions, finely chopped
6 strips lemon rind,
   thinly sliced
30 ml butter
30 ml cake flour
roasted sesame seeds
   and chopped parsley
   for garnishing

yellowtail and cucumber kebab

Vissermans Kombuis,
Paternoster, West Coast

1 kg yellowtail fillets
1 large English cucumber,
   halved lengthwise and
   deseeded
1 large green, yellow or
   red pepper
1 onion

marinade
150 ml dry white wine
10 ml sugar
60 g melted butter
30 ml chopped fresh
   rosemary

Cut yellowtail fillets into 4 cm cubes. Cut cucumber into 30 mm chunks and divide green, yellow or red pepper and onion into 8 pieces each (use different colour peppers if available). Arrange fish, cucumber, peppers and onions on the skewer in repetitive order. Put kebabs into a container and pour over marinade. Refrigerate for 1–2 hours.

Grill over medium heat, basting regularly. Serve with chips or rice.

wine suggestion
Weskus Blanc de Blanc

Serves 4

tannie evita se 'koeksusters'

Evita se Perron,
Darling Station

For the syrup, boil the sugar, water, flavouring, cream of tartar and tartaric acid until it syrups, approximately 10 minutes. Set aside to cool.

For the dough, sift the dry ingredients. Lightly cut or rub the margarine into the dry ingredients. Beat the egg well and mix in the milk. Add egg and milk mixture to flour mixture, handling as little as possible. Refrigerate for at least 1 hour. Roll out the dough to a thickness of 4 mm and cut into strips 8 cm long and 2.5 cm wide. Cut each strip lengthwise into two or three strips, leaving one short side uncut. Twist or plait the loose pieces and press ends together firmly. Deep fry in hot oil until golden brown. Dip hot koeksisters into cool syrup, drain and cool. Koeksisters can be stored in the refrigerator for up to one week.

Serve with filter coffee.

makes 10–15

syrup
1 kg sugar
500 ml water
5 ml vanilla essence or
    grated orange rind or
    ground cinnamon
1.5 ml ground ginger
5 ml cream of tartar
2.5 ml tartaric acid

dough
500 ml cake flour
10 ml baking powder
5 ml salt
70 ml margarine
1 egg
80 ml milk

oil for frying

cape coon carnival

kalk bay

the cape
peninsula
& winelands

hex river valley   table mountain

The Cape Peninsula, the mother city of Cape Town and the outlying winelands hold undeniable allure for the visitor. There is glamour, elegance, culture, history and, best of all, unlimited opportunities for high-quality leisure and recreation. The city is stylish, laid back, trend-setting, its three million people an interesting cosmopolitan mix.

The city lies in the shelter of one of the world's most famous landmarks, the 350 million-year-old massif that is Table Mountain, overlooking the sheltered waters of Table Bay. Beyond its boundaries are the highlands of the Boland, a golden land of wheat, fruit and wine to accompany the bounty of the two great oceans lapping its shores.

Many of the city's cultural and historical attractions are in the centre, accessible on foot. Historic Government Avenue cuts a swathe through the six-hectare Company's Garden, 17th century larder of the Dutch East India Company, past the Cultural History Museum, St George's Cathedral, the Houses of Parliament, the South African Library, the State President's 1701 residence, Tuynhuis, South Africa's oldest synagogue and the National Gallery with its gleaming copper-domed planetarium.

Strand, Keerom, Burg, Buitenkant and Buitengracht streets display elegant 18th and 19th century architecture, while Greenmarket Square, once a market for farmers' produce, is an exciting venue for crafters and buskers. Long Street has a New Orleans feel with

Above: The flower markets in Adderley Street and on the Grand Parade in Cape Town are a feast for the eyes. Vendors jostle with one another to offer the best bargains of the day, with prices descending as the sun goes down.

Opposite: South Africa's national flower, the king protea (Protea cynaroides), is one of 6 000 indigenous species of flora found in the national botanic garden at Kirstenbosch. The gardens, laid out over 528 hectares on the eastern slopes of Table Mountain, attract half a million visitors a year.

Above: Noordhoek is one of the longest of the 50 beaches surrounding the Cape Peninsula. It lies in a generous curve beyond the pretty fishing harbour and village of Hout Bay.

ornate Victorian buildings housing antique shops and rare bookstores. Kloof Street is Cape Town's unofficial restaurant district, where it's possible to order anything from the freshest fish and chips in a basket, to European haute cuisine. The Bo-Kaap, on the slopes of Signal Hill, preserves the heritage of Cape Town's early Cape Malay citizens, a community of skilled craftspeople who brought a wealth of culture and their unique cuisine to the Cape.

A special excursion should be made to the 325-year-old Castle of Good Hope, earliest base of the Dutch East India Company and one of the best-preserved of all remaining Dutch

East India Company forts. It was just next door, on the historic Grand Parade that Nelson Mandela addressed the world in February 1990, shortly after his release from Robben Island.

Five minutes west of the city centre, the V&A Waterfront is Cape Town's premier consumer playground, developed around a picturesque working harbour. The Waterfront is a mecca for round-the-clock shopping, eating and entertainment, with a maritime museum, luxury hotels, and a world-class aquarium.

The southern peninsula is composed of a line of pleasant, leafy suburbs linked to the city by Rhodes Drive. The drive sweeps past the renowned heart-transplant hospital, Groote Schuur, and the University of Cape Town, beautiful Kirstenbosch National Botanic Gardens, to the suburb of Constantia, home of South Africa's oldest wine estate.

The Cape Peninsula is 70 kilometres in length from the city centre to the nature reserve at Cape Point, with at least 50 beaches along its 150 kilometres of coastline. The sandy beach at Noordhoek is one of the longest beaches in the world, said to be second in length only to Acapulco! The protected warm-water beaches of False Bay, including Muizenberg, are perhaps the most appealing to the visitor, who may find a plunge into the icy waters of Clifton on the western peninsula a dash too challenging. Legend has it that the two oceans meet at the stormy tip of the windblown peninsula – a romantic notion gainsaid by pedants who deem the meeting-place to be 200 km eastwards, at Cape Agulhas.

Below: Cape Point, the southernmost tip of the Peninsula, is the mythological meeting place of the Indian and Atlantic Ocean, said to be clearly indicated by the white line of foam extending seawards. Overleaf: Table Mountain in classically beautiful pose seen from Blouberg's beach.

From the oldest cellars at Groot Constantia, the Cape's winelands expanded over three centuries to the towns of Stellenbosch and Franschhoek in the immediate hinterland or Boland, and beyond, to a total of 13 regions spreading hundreds of kilometres as far north as the Orange River. The Boland's wines accompany delicious regional dishes, most notably the fragrant 'bredies', such as 'waterblommetjies' (*Aponogeton distachyos*) slow-cooked with knuckle or neck of mutton and enhanced with nutmeg and sorrel. The Boland's premier social event is the annual Nederberg wine auction, first held in 1975.

Right: *The great estate of Boschendal at Franschhoek is among 14 wine producing farms in the area. The* Vignerons de Franschhoek *uphold noble French wine-making traditions introduced by the Huguenots, who settled here in 1688. The manor house is an exquisite example of an H-shaped Cape Dutch farmhouse, and holds a priceless collection of 17th-century porcelain.*

Left: The 300-year-old Lanzerac Manor and Winery at Stellenbosch is synonymous with the tradition of Cape hospitality – the finest food and shelter under one roof, accompanied, of course, by outstanding local wines.

Below: Vergelegen estate is the pride of the Helderberg wine region. Its beautiful gardens draw visitors year round, to admire its flowers or to stand in the shade of its majestic camphor trees.

crayfish samoosas set on a vegetable chutney

Bosman's at Grand Roche Paarl

samoosas

6 sheets of spring roll
    pastry, each 15 x 15 cm
4 crayfish tails, cooked and
    cut into small cubes
20 coriander leaves,
    finely chopped
15 ml finely diced fresh
    ginger
salt and pepper to taste
1 egg yolk, whisked
500 ml oil for deep frying

chutney

30 coriander leaves,
    finely chopped
15 mint leaves, finely
    chopped
135 ml dark brown sugar
180 ml raspberry vinegar
salt and pepper
125 ml mango purée
120 g carrot, julienned
120 g leek, julienned
120 g baby marrow,
    julienned
120 g pineapple, julienned

For the samoosas, cut each sheet of spring roll pastry into four strips, 3.5 cm wide. Mix the crayfish, coriander and ginger together and season with salt and pepper to taste. Divide the crayfish mixture between the 24 strips of springroll pastry and fold each into a triangular shape. Close the triangles with a thin layer of egg yolk. Fry the samoosas in the preheated oil for about 2 minutes. Drain on a kitchen towel.

For the chutney, mix the coriander, mint, brown sugar, raspberry vinegar, salt, pepper and mango purée in a food processor. Quickly blanch the julienned vegetables in boiling water and refresh in ice water to strengthen the colour. Caramelise the coriander mixture in a cast-iron skillet. Add the prepared vegetables and pineapple and sauté until al the liquid has evaporated.

To serve, spoon a pool of vegetable chutney onto each plate and top with three samoosas per serving.

serves 8

wine suggestion
Stellenzicht Semillon Reserve

grilled franschhoek smoked salmon trout on sautéd new potatoes with mixed leaves, tomato concasse and watercress dressing

Haute Cabriére Cellar Restaurant,
Franschhoek

For the dressing, sauté the onion, garlic and apple in the oil. Add wine and fish stock. Reduce by half and add cream. Reduce slightly more. Blend watercress and spinach, then add reduced cream sauce. Blend quickly, pass through a fine sieve, add balsamic vinegar, and salt and pepper to taste.

For the salmon trout, lightly dust the fish with flour. Grill the portions in olive oil on a hot skillet or flat-topped grill for 1–2 minutes, leaving them slightly underdone in the middle.

To serve, sauté the new potatoes in clarified butter, tossing them occasionally to get an even, brown color. Toss the salad greens in vinaigrette. Place the potatoes on the plate, top with salmon. Surround with watercress dressing, top with salad greens and sprinkle on the diced tomato and caviar.

serves 4

wine suggestion
Pierre Jordaan Cuvée Belle Rose

Watercress dressing
½ onion, chopped
2 cloves garlic, peeled and chopped
1 apple, peeled, cored and chopped
10 ml oil
125 ml white wine
100 ml reduced fish stock
500 ml cream
400 g watercress
100 g spinach
50 ml balsamic vinegar
salt and pepper

salmon trout
4 x 100 g portions Franschhoek smoked salmon trout, cut thick from a side
15 ml cake flour
40 ml virgin olive oil

to serve
400 g new potatoes, boiled, peeled and cut into wedges
50 ml clarified butter
150 g mixed salad leaves and herbs (8 or more different kinds)
2 medium tomatoes, peeled seeded and diced
30 ml vinaigrette dressing
50 g salmon caviar

baked rack of lamb with a tomato and sage crust, served on seared spinach

Die Ou Pastorie,
Somerset West

1 small tin tomato paste
250 g bread crumbs
2 fresh tomatoes, skinned,
    seeded and diced
100 g butter
20 g fresh sage, chopped,
    or 10 g dried
salt and pepper
4 racks of lamb, with 3 ribs
    each, well trimmed
15 ml olive oil
400 ml cream
100 g mild wholegrain
    mustard
2 bunches of spinach,
    stalks removed and
    washed thoroughly,
    roughly chopped
freshly cut mixed herbs,
    chopped

Preheat the oven to 200 °C. Mix together the tomato paste, bread crumbs, tomatoes, butter, sage, salt and pepper to form the crust. Season the lamb racks and quickly sear in a hot pan with a little olive oil. Place in an oven roasting dish. Top each rack with 1/4 of the crust mixture. Place in the preheated oven for 7–10 minutes for medium-rare, or 10–15 minutes for medium.

Place the cream and mustard in a saucepan and simmer together for 5 minutes. Set aside and keep warm.

In the pan used to seal the lamb, sauté the spinach at a very high heat until heated, but not wilted. Divide the spinach into four portions and place in the middle of warmed plates.

Place a portion of lamb on top of each mound of spinach and pour some of the mustard cream sauce around the spinach. Garnish with fresh herbs.

serves 4

wine suggestion
Bodega Cabernet Sauvignon

roasted fillet of springbok with sweet potato dauphinoise, fresh berries, caremelised baby corn and gooseberry jus

Prepare the potatoes well in advance – this allows them to firm up for easier cutting. Parboil the potatoes whole, allow to cool and then slice thinly. Sweat the onion and garlic together. Layer the potato, sweet potato, cream, and onion and garlic mix alternately in a greased baking tray. Layer until the potato is about 5 cm thick. Seaon with nutmeg, salt and pepper. Bake in a preheated oven at 180 °C for 1/2 hour. Allow to cool, then place a weight on the potato tray to compress the potato. Cut out with a cookie cutter and reheat for 20 minutes before serving.

Seal the meat quickly on a hot grill then place in the oven to roast at 180 °C until medium rare.

For the sauce, sweat the onion and garlic, then deglaze the pan with Ratafia. Add the reduced stock and cream and boil until reduced by a third for the sauce.

Cut the baby corn into lengths and caramelize in the honey. Do the same with the berries.

To serve, spoon some sauce onto a warmed plate. Place a poato round in the middle of the plate and arrange the sliced meat to the side. Spoon the berries around the potato and meat, and top the potato with baby corn.

serves 4

wine suggestion
Haute Cabrière Pinot Noir

Haute Cabriére
Cellar Restaurant,
Franschhoek

**sweet potato
dauphinoise**
500 g potatoes
500 g sweet potatoes
½ onion, chopped
2 cloves garlic, chopped
400 ml cream
grated nutmeg
salt and pepper

springbok
4 x 200 g-portions
springbok (or equivalent),
cut from the loin

sauce
½ onion
5 ml chopped garlic
100 ml olive oil
dash of Ratafia
250 ml reduced venison
stock
100 ml cream

to serve
200 g baby corn
100 ml honey
200 g gooseberries
200 g mixed berries
(blue, black, raspberries,
and youngberries)

cardamom and clove spiced duck breasts

Franschhoek Country House, Franschhoek

4 duck breasts
60 ml crushed cardamom
30 ml crushed cloves
1 packet Udon noodles
65 ml olive oil
180 ml sweet soya sauce
250 ml clarified butter
2 lemons, cut into segments
125 ml preserved ginger (with syrup)
2 bunches spring onions, cut into rounds
1½ leeks, shredded and deep fried
salt and pepper to taste

Preheat the oven to 300 °C. Coat the duck with cardomom and clove mixture. Soak the noodles in cold water for 10 minutes. Cook in boiling water for 4 minutes and strain. Heat the olive oil until hot in a pan, then fry the duck breasts on the skin side first for 1 minute, then turn over and fry for about 10 seconds. Reduce the heat and fry skin side down for another minute, being careful not to burn the skin. Brush with sweet soya sauce, then place skin-side up on a baking tray in the preheated oven. Cook for another 2 minutes, for medium-rare duck.

Heat butter in a pan. Add the noodles and fry until crispy. Heat lemon segments and ginger in preserved ginger syrup. Blanch the spring onions in boiling water, Fry in clarified butter and season.

To assemble, arrange crispy noodles in the centre of a plate and top with spring onions. Slice the duck breasts and arrange on one side of the noodles. Cover duck with lemon and ginger. Douse with sweet soya sauce and top with deep-fried leeks.

serves 4

wine suggestion
Glen Carlou Oak Matured Chardonnay

panna cotta with brown sugar and vanilla bean

Franschhoek
Country House,
Franschhoek

In a large saucepan over low heat bring the cream, milk
and vanilla to the boil. Set aside to infuse for 20 minutes.
Sprinkle the gelatine into the water and allow to sponge.
Scrape the seeds from the vanilla pod and whisk into the
cream mixture. Return to the stove. Add the castor sugar
and heat, stirring occasionally, until the mixture is almost
boiling. Remove from the heat and add the gelatine,
stirring until dissolved. Set aside to cool, or, to chill quickly,
stir over ice.

When the mixture is cool and just beginning to set,
strain into a clean bowl and whisk to distribute the vanilla
seeds evenly through the mixture. Pour into 8 lightly oiled
250 ml moulds, cover and refrigerate until set.

For the syrup, heat all the ingredients over medium heat,
stirring occasionally, until the mixture simmers. Reduce
heat and simmer gently for 30 minutes. Scrape the seeds
from the vanilla pod and whisk into the syrup. Leave the
vanilla pod and the zest to infuse in the syrup, and allow
to cool. Pour the syrup into an airtight container and
refrigerate until required.

To assemble, turn each Panna Cotta out onto an
individual plate, and serve with a little thick cream and a
generous serving of the syrup.

serves 8

wine suggestion
Pierre Jordaan Ratafia

panna cotta
750 ml cream
750 ml milk
1 vanilla pod, split
45 ml gelatine
125 ml water
125 ml castor sugar

syrup
500 ml water
375 ml dark brown sugar
3 strips lemon zest
1 vanilla pod, split
pinch of salt

to serve
thick cream

mille feuille of winter pastry leaves
and lemon parfait with a compôte of berries

The Atlantic Grill at
The Table Bay Hotel,
Cape Town

puff pastry leaves
250 g butter puff paste
    or scrap that has been
    folded once
icing sugar

lemon parfait
500 ml cream
juice of 5 lemons
zest of 1 lemon
8 egg yolks
225 ml sugar
115 ml water

champagne sabayon
1 egg
1 egg yolk
30 ml castor sugar
1 gelatine leaf, softened
    in a little water
350 ml double cream
15 ml champagne

to serve
lemon zest
fresh mint leaves

mille feuille
100 ml raspberry coulis
50 ml blackberry coulis
400 g blueberries,
    strawberries and
    raspberries, washed
    and hulled

For the puff pastry leaves, instead of using flour to roll out the pastry, use sifted icing sugar. Roll out as thinly as possible, lightly dusting as you go. Roll up tightly to form a long cigar and leave to rest for 1 hour. Cut disks off the cigar and again using the icing sugar mixture, roll these out into a circle, as thin as possible. Transfer to a baking sheet or silicone paper and bake at 180 °C for about 10 minutes, then turn and bake until the sugar has caramelised and is a deep golden brown. Remove to cool on a wire rack.

For the lemon parfait, whisk the cream to soft peak and refrigerate. In a stainless-steel pot reduce the lemon juice by two-thirds. Whisk the yolks over simmering water until thick and pale. Remove from the heat. Bring the sugar and water to the boil and continue to cook until it reaches soft ball stage. Using an electric mixer, whisk the sabayon while adding the sugar syrup in a slow, continuous stream. Add the lemon juice and zest and continue to beat until cool. Remove from mixer and refrigerate until cold. Fold the cream gently through the lemon sabayon and pour into appropriate moulds or terrine form and freeze.

For the champagne sabayon, mix the egg and egg yolk with the sugar in a bowl over a bain marie until warm, then allow to cool. Add the softened gelatine to the egg mixture and mix in well. Whip the double cream to firm peaks, whisk in the champagne, then fold into the egg mixture. Chill for 30 minutes.

Keep a few berries aside for garnish and mix the rest in a bowl, together with about half the champagne sabayon. To serve, spoon some coulis onto each plate. Place a puff pastry disc on the coulis, and top with a disc of lemon parfait. Place another puff pastry disc on top. Onto that, spoon some mixed berries, dust with a little icing sugar and decorate with lemon zest, mint and retained berries.

wine suggestion
Nederburg Edelkeur

cango valley, oudtshoorn

great karoo

karoo
& northern cape

augrabies falls national park

quiver tree

This is the land of broad brushstrokes – wide horizons, high skies and vast plains. Everything is huge. Farms run to thousands of kilometres in extent, and the tiny towns are sparsely distributed, lying hundreds of kilometres apart. It is a place to breathe, and to stand in awe of nature's limitless generosity.

Not only are the landscapes unforgettable in their expanse, but nature has bestowed upon this earth diamonds, fossils and specialised crops such as olives, cotton and dates. There are grapes to make sweet wine. Its well-nourished animals produce beautiful mohair, prized karakul pelts, and, for the table, mutton made aromatic with natural herbs. Most of South Africa's top racehorses are bred here, and it is home to the world's biggest bird – the fast, aggressive, flightless ostrich.

Two of South Africa's great natural assets are located in the northern Cape. The Augrabies Falls National Park protects the biggest granite gorge on earth, while the Kgalagadi Transfrontier Park is a specialised habitat for the stately desert antelope, *Oryx gazella*.

Above: The reclusive artist Helen Martens left a store of brooding artworks in her cottage, The Owl House, in the eastern Karoo town of Nieu-Bethesda. The house and its garden are filled with cement sculptures, which include life-sized camels, peacocks and owls.

Opposite: The biggest of all living bird species is the flightless ostrich. Its huge wings are used for balance while running, or to provide shelter and protection while hatching eggs. Both parents tend the nest – the black male at night, the grey female by day. The eggs take 42 days to incubate and one is equivalent in volume to 24 hens' eggs.

The Karoo and northern Cape occupy much of South Africa's central plateau, measuring roughly 400 000 square kilometres or almost half the extent of the country. Named Karoo by the Bushmen who roamed these 'dry and dusty plains', the charms of this harsh stretch of land are discreet but seductive, as writers Sir Lourens van der Post, Lawrence Green and Olive Schreiner have described in their literature.

It is wholly appropriate that this imposing plateauland be entered through ceremonial gateways, in this instance, two spectacular gorges and an awesome mountain pass on its southern threshold. The historic Swartberg, Meiringspoort and Seweweekspoort passes were chiselled by man out of rock, to make pathways for trade through the mountain barrier. The Swartberg Pass, with its astonishing rock formations and rich bird life and plant life, is considered one of the great ecodestinations in the country. At the northern foot of the pass a tiny historic village, Prince Albert, provides an ideal base for exploring the mountains and the secret valley of Gamkaskloof, also known as 'The Hell', where the small self-sufficient community lived in isolation for more than 100 years.

Below: *A cheetah* (Acinonyx jubatus) *focuses on its prey in the great wilderness of the Kgalagadi Transfrontier Park. Black-maned lion and leopard are also among the park's large population of predators. Among the many species of antelope is its namesake, the majestic gemsbok* (Oryx gazella).

It is in the peaceful towns of the platteland that old-style South African hospitality, and most of its traditional cuisine, lives on. Here nothing is hurried, and the great expanses offer the traveller an unrivalled atmosphere of serenity in which to open his senses and rest a while.

While most of the early settlements dozed sleepily on through the centuries, the 1800s brought unexpected wealth, in the form of ostrich feathers and diamonds, to two small towns at opposite ends of the region: Oudtshoorn in the far south, and Kimberley way to the north.

The little Karoo village of Oudtshoorn gave rise to sandstone 'palaces' built by ostrich-feather barons made rich by European fashion. Tourists flocked to see the big, strange birds, and the now world-famous Cango Caves. Kimberley's diamond legacy lives on in the world's biggest mining house, De Beers, which still has its headquarters in the 'Big Hole' town. It was here, too, that Cecil John Rhodes and Barney Barnato rubbed shoulders with Dr Leander Starr Jameson, whose historic raid precipitated the bitter Anglo-Boer war.

Some of Kimberley's most important military history is preserved in the McGregor Museum,

Rhodes' home during the Siege of Kimberley. There are other significant war sites throughout the region, including Colesberg, Burgersdorp, Bethulie and Matjiesfontein.

It is impossible to explore every part of this historic and fascinating region of the country, but there are several more detours to be made, starting with the towns, resorts and nature reserves round the two major water-sources for the region, one natural and one man-made, namely the Orange River, and the Gariep Dam.

Upington is the most prominent of the settlements on the verdant southern bank of the Orange River. The town commands the entire Orange River Valley, which, thanks to extensive irrigation, has become richly productive. River safaris and campouts under the stars are a wonderful way to experience the lazy reaches of the huge river, and to admire the almost lunar quality of the Kalahari landscapes on its northern banks.

Above: The Victorian Lord Milner Hotel at Matjiesfontein on the Blue Train route from Cape Town to Pretoria. The tiny settlement is best known as the one-time home of South Africa's 'founder' writer, Olive Schreiner, who retreated here regularly to relieve her asthma in the dry Karoo air.

baked fresh figs with gorgonzola

Andries Stockenström Guesthouse, Graaff-Reinet

4 large (or 8 small) fresh figs
120 g gorgonzola cheese
60 ml roasted and finely chopped almonds
4 slices white bread
olive oil
mixed salad leaves
salad dressing

Cut off and retain the top third of each fig. Form the cheese into 4 small balls and roll it in the almonds. Make a small hole in the larger section of the fig and press the cheese ball into the hole. From a slice of white bread cut a round big enough to use as a base for the fig, and dab with olive oil. Place the fig on the bread, replace the top of the fig and brush the whole fig with olive oil. Place on a baking sheet and bake in a preheated oven at 180 °C until the cheese begins to melt. While the fig is baking, arrange salad leaves in the centre of a plate and drizzle with salad dressing. Place the fig on top and serve immediately.

serves 4

wine suggestion
Monis Pale Dry Sherry

tartare of ostrich fillet with olive oil

Bernard se Taphuis, Oudtshoorn

200 g ostrich fillet, finely
    chopped or minced
2 ml salt
freshly ground white pepper
1 clove garlic
pinch of whole caraway
    chopped with olive oil
15 ml finely chopped
    parsley
1 small pickled cucumber
2 small escholottel brunoise,
    or other small, mild onions
pinch of chilli or tabasco
30 ml olive oil
2 ml paprika
4 pickled capers, chopped

1 anchovy fillet, chopped
a dash of lemon juice
2 ml hot mustard

garnish
onion rings, parsley and chives
4 raw egg yolks, in shell

Mix all the ingredients with the minced meat. Divide meat into 4 portions and serve, garnished with onion rings, parsley, chives and a raw egg yolk in its shell. Serve with a fresh hot baguette and butter, and in hot weather, with iced beef tea.

serves 4

wine suggestion
Saxenburg Shiraz

spinach and cheese soup

The Victoria Room, Swartberg Country Lodge, Prince Albert

500 ml cooked spinach
125 ml chopped onion,
    sautéd
500 ml thick béchamel
    sauce
250 ml full-cream milk
salt and freshly ground
    black pepper to taste

to serve
cream
125 ml grated mature
    cheddar cheese
paprika

Finely chop the spinach and onions in a food processor. Heat the béchamel sauce in a saucepan until boiling point. Stir in the spinach mixture and milk and simmer until well heated. Season to taste and thin with more milk if necessary.

    To serve, garnish with a swirl of cream, a croûton topped with grated cheddar cheese and a sprinkling of paprika.

serves 6

wine suggestion
Savanna Dry Wooded Chenin Blanc

tartare of ostrich fillet with olive oil

spinach and cheese soup

loin of karoo mutton in a herb crust with red wine and garlic sauce

Andries Stockenström Guesthouse, Graaff-Reinet

1 loin of mutton,
    sinews and excess fat
    removed, ± 800 g
salt and pepper
300 ml fine breadcrumbs
250 ml chopped fresh
    parsley
10 ml chopped fresh thyme
10 ml chopped fresh
    rosemary
10 ml chopped garlic
125 ml olive oil
2 egg whites, lightly beaten
butter

red wine sauce
300 ml dark brown stock
375 ml red wine
180 ml port wine
salt to taste
50 g unsalted butter, chilled

garlic sauce
250 ml fresh cream
125 ml fresh garlic cloves,
    peeled and trimmed
salt and pepper

to serve
rosemary sprigs

Preheat oven to 190 °C. Season the loin with salt and pepper. Mix the breadcrumbs, herbs, garlic and enough olive oil to moisten, and cover the loin with the mixture. If the breadcrumbs are coarse, pulp the mixture in a blender. Brush egg white on the fat-covered side of the loin and pat on the breadcrumb mixture. Heat some of the olive oil and a knob of butter in a frying pan and when hot, add the loin and seal on each side. Roast in the oven for 15–20 minutes or more if preferred. Remove and rest for 5 minutes.

For the red wine sauce, mix the stock, red wine and port in a large saucepan. Reduce slowly to 500 ml (the sauce can be prepared the previous day up to this stage, reheated and finished). Season with salt and thicken by beating in small knobs of the chilled butter.

For the garlic sauce, simmer the garlic cloves very slowly in the cream until soft – about 45 minutes. Press through a sieve and season with salt and pepper. Keep in the refrigerator if prepared beforehand and reheat before serving.

To serve, cut the loin diagonally in thick slices. Pour enough red wine sauce onto each plate to almost cover the centre of the plate. Spoon some of the garlic sauce in the middle, and arrange three slices of meat on each plate. Garnish with a sprig of rosemary and serve hot.

serves 4

wine suggestion
Klein Constantia Cabernet

ostrich egg soufflé salzburger style

Bernard se Taphuis, Oudtshoorn

Separate egg white and yolk. Butter a cocotte or other oval ovenproof dish. Wash strawberries and halve them, then lay them out in the buttered dish. Sprinkle icing sugar over the strawberries and then sprinkle with Cointreau.

Now beat all the egg white with sugar, vanilla sugar, salt and lemon juice until fluffy. Fold one-third of the egg yolk into the egg white, taking care not to overfold. Form into three 'mountains' over the strawberries and bake in the oven at 170 °C for about 20 minutes. Sprinkle with icing sugar and serve immediately.

serves 6

wine suggestion
Twee Jongegezellen or
Krone Borealis sparkling wine

1 medium ostrich egg
10 ml butter
200 g strawberries
125 ml icing sugar
50 ml Cointreau
120 ml sugar
10 ml vanilla sugar
5 ml salt
dash of lemon juice

garnish
icing sugar

'armmans' pudding

The Victoria Room,
Swartberg Country
Lodge, Prince Albert

This is a well-known regional dessert and a favourite with overseas visitors. It is based on a recipe for brandy pudding, but made without the brandy – hence the name 'armmans' (poor man's) pudding.

6 eggs
500 ml sugar
500 ml cake flour
10 ml baking soda
500 ml lukewarm milk
125 ml smooth apricot jam
125 g softened butter
2 ml lemon juice

syrup
250 ml sugar
250 ml cream
250 g butter
10 ml vanilla essence
750 ml boiling water

to serve
thick cream

Whisk the eggs and sugar together.
Sift the flour and baking soda into this
mixture. Slowly add the milk and mix
well. Mix the apricot jam, butter and lemon
juice together and add to the egg mixture.
Pour the batter into a medium-sized
ovenproof dish about 5 cm deep, then
bake at 180 °C forabout 35 minutes,
or until a skewer inserted in the centre
comes out clean.
   In a saucepan, mix all the ingredients for
the syrup and heat. Pour slowly over the
pudding. Serve warm with thick cream.

serves 8

wine suggestion
Lieveland Noble Late Harvest

waenhuiskrans   wilderness lagoon

garden route, overberg & eastern cape

tsitsikamma national park

outeniqua tjoe-choo

Long-ago settlers at the tip of Africa gazed towards the 'mountains of Africa' and imagined that fabulous wealth lay just beyond their distant blue ridges in the empire of Monomotapa. In a sense, they were right. It is a gold and azure land of undulating hills and valleys, lofty skies, long, deserted beaches and the warm blue waters of the Indian Ocean. Small wonder that many of South Africa's favourite holiday destinations are along the southern and eastern Cape coast, with the Garden Route – 300 kilometres of beaches and seaside resorts, mountains and forests, lakes and lagoons – right in the centre.

The entire region is blessed with temperate weather, its landscapes are a balm for the soul, and there's plenty to eat and drink. The Overberg is the larder of the Cape, producing abundant wheat, fruit, wine, mutton and beef, to complement a huge variety of seafood from the coast. The southern and eastern Cape coasts yield mammoth oysters, mussels, calamari and a delectable variety of linefish, as well as the rigorously protected perlemoen (abalone).

The southern Cape coast is also on the 900-kilometre whale route, which spans two oceans and sweeps past their meeting point at Agulhas, the southernmost tip of the African continent. The Overberg town of Hermanus, just an hour's drive from Cape Town, is considered one of the top 13 whale-watching sites in the world. Each year from May to November, southern right whales come into Walker Bay to mate and calve, attracting thousands of visitors to the resort.

Above: The bustling town of George lies at the foothills of the Outeniqua Mountains, which form the first barrier between the coastal terrace and the interior. Blessed with lavish rainfall, the town gardens – like this one surrounding the 1842 Dutch Reformed Church – are showpieces. Outeniqua translates from the San language as 'man laden with honey'.

Opposite: The immense beach at Wilderness unfolds in breathtaking vista from a viewsite at Dolphin's Point on the N2 highway through the Garden Route. The bathing beach of Leentjiesklip is in the foreground. From the point the road drops rapidly to sea level, taking travellers on towards the resort towns of Knysna and Plettenberg Bay.

When the whales are not at play, there are plenty of other things to do around the coastal resorts and their inland neighbours. Sportsmen are indulged with splendid golf courses, sailing and all manner of watersports, hiking, walking, riding and fishing, while ecotourists can head for any one of dozens of reserves inland or along the coast. The lagoons, lakes, vleis, estuaries and in some places, the shoreline and the adjacent waters are proteced by a series of contiguous sanctuaries along the southern and eastern coasts, including the Tsitsikamma Coastal National Park, and the Knysna National Lake Area. The popular Otter Trail provides visitors the opportunity to explore, on foot, all the mystical places and hidden secrets of the Tsitsikamma park.

The Garden Route meets the Eastern Cape at a spectacular bridge over the Storms River gorge, entry to the Sunshine Coast with its capital, the friendly city of Port Elizabeth. The cities and towns of the Eastern Cape move at a different pace from their western sisters. Much smaller and altogether more leisurely than Cape Town, Port Elizabeth, far removed from the Mother City, retains something of the air of a border town. And herein lies much of its charm. Its proximity to the traditional Xhosa territories gives it an African flavour that combines vibrantly with its strong

Opposite: Known as The Heads, a massive pair of sandstone bluffs protects the entrance to Knysna's sheltered lagoon. The western bluff shown here, is undeveloped, home only to a private nature reserve, which shelters birds and the rare blue duiker. Beyond the western promontory is the holiday resort of Brenton-on-Sea.

Right: The Cango Caves in the Swartberg are considered to be among the best examples of limestone caves in the world. Threatened by exposure to light and the constant chipping of small souvenirs by millions of tourists a year, the future management of the caves is under urgent review. Cango One, the first of four sequences, presents an awesome series of 28 chambers criss-crossed by 2.4 kilometres of passageways.

Right: *Hermanus, once a sleepy fishing village, has become a sophisticated holiday resort where the rich and famous rub elbows each summer. Real estate prices are as high as Johannesburg and Cape Town – due in no small part to its increasing renown as a top site for whale-watching. Each year, southern right whales come into the shelter of Walker Bay to mate and calve for six months from May to November.*

British heritage passed down from the 4 000 British settlers who were brought to Port Elizabeth in 1820, with a brief to establish farms and provide an informal garrison on the frontier. Their vision of a new life was shattered when they were swiftly caught up in bloody territorial conflicts that lasted for 100 years. Their descendents still form the backbone of the Eastern Cape, both in town and country where family farms have been handed down through generations. The city of Port Elizabeth has preserved much of its Victorian colonial architecture and statuary – there is a fine example of Queen Victoria in Sicilian marble on the Market Square – and boasts numerous gothic and art nouveau buildings.

Grahamstown, the City of Saints and of Scholars, is about an hour by road north east of Port Elizabeth in the heart of 1820 Settler country. Named for its 40 churches, fine schools and historic Rhodes University, Grahamstown is also host to the annual national arts festival held over the course of a week in June.

Below: *Plettenberg Bay, 250 kilometres to the east, ranks with Hermanus as one of the country's top coastal destinations. 'Plett', as it is affectionately known to locals and regulars, was once a Norwegian whaling station, but today provides these great mammals with sanctuary. Robberg beach is one of three near the town. Its peninsula, far left of the picture, has three early burial sites with finds dating back to 700 BC.*

spicy prawn and coconut cream soup

**The Med
Seafood Bistro,
Plettenberg Bay**

15 ml oil
2 cloves garlic
3 small onions, chopped
3 small red chillies, chopped
20 ml snipped fresh lemon grass
4 ml shrimp paste
2 chicken stock cubes, crumbled and dissolved in
750 ml boiling water
500 g orange pumpkin, diced
400 ml coconut cream
15 ml cornflour mixed with a little cold water
250 g small cooked prawns
15 ml shredded basil

Heat oil in a pan, add the garlic, onions, chillies, lemon
grass and shrimp paste and cook until the onions are
soft. Add the stock and bring to the boil. Add the
pumpkin and simmer for 10 minutes or until the
pumpkin is soft. Mash the pumpkin slightly with a fork.
Stir in the coconut cream and cornflour mixture and
heat through. Add the prawns, and stir until heated
through. Serve sprinkled with shredded basil.

serves 4

wine suggestion
Haute Cabriere Chardonnay Pinot Noir

springbok carpaccio with roasted peppers in balsamic dressing

The Cock House, Grahamstown

4 x 40 g portions smoked
    springbok, sliced
    paper thin
mixed salad leaves and
    mixed herbs

roasted peppers
1 each green, red and
    yellow pepper
100 ml olive oil
15 ml balsamic vinegar
15 ml lemon juice
2 ml crushed garlic
5 ml chopped fresh
    origanum
5 ml chopped fresh basil
salt and freshly ground
    black pepper

Roast the peppers on a baking tray under a hot grill and keep turning until the skin is blackened. Place in a plastic bag, tie the bag and leave to cool, then open the bag and remove the skins. Cut the peppers in half, remove the seeds and slice the peppers lengthways into strips. For the dressing, combine all the other ingredients. Lay the peppers in a single layer in a shallow dish, pour over the dressing, cover and chill.

To serve, garnish the plate with mixed salad leaves and fresh herbs. Lay out a portion of the springbok with fanned slices of marinated peppers. Drizzle a little dressing from the marinade over the springbok slices.

serves 4

wine suggestion
Louisvale Chavant Chardonnay

beef fillet medallions with port and mushroom sauce

Greyton Lodge, Greyton

4 beef fillet medallions
15 ml sunflower oil

sauce
100 ml port
150 ml chopped
    mushrooms
250 ml brown stock
125 ml cream
salt and freshly ground
    black pepper

Heat the oil in a frying pan. Fry the beef fillets for three minutes on each side over high heat. Remove fillets from heat and keep warm. (Fillets must be pink on the inside.) Add port, mushrooms, stock and cream and cook over medium heat until slightly thickened. Season with salt and pepper. Serve each fillet on a pool of port and mushroom sauce.

serves 4

wine suggestion
Diemersdal Shiraz

beef fillet medallions
with port and mushroom sauce

springbok carpaccio with roasted
peppers in balsamic dressing

shredded duck with thai noodles

The Cock House
Grahamstown

This recipe is
adapted from
*Open Rhodes
Around Britain*
by Gary Rhodes.

1 whole duck, giblets removed
   and cut into 4 portions
salt
500 g white fat, melted
2 whole garlic cloves, peeled

noodles
3 bundles of tagliatelle per person
10 ml sunflower oil
a few torn fresh mint and
   coriander leaves

noodle sauce
75 ml white wine vinegar
45 ml fish sauce
120 ml olive oil
1 large garlic clove, crushed

5 ml fresh ginger, finely chopped
juice and grated rind of half an
   orange and half a lemon
1 or 2 red chillies with seeds,
   finely chopped
freshly ground black pepper
10 ml finely chopped lemon grass
10 ml finely chopped fresh coriander
   leaves with stalks

duck sauce
10 ml melted fat from cooked duck
10 ml cake flour
juice of half an orange
duck stock
5 ml Triple Sec

To prepare the duck, preheat the oven to 175 °C. Rub salt over the outer skin of the duck portions. Melt the fat in a large heavy-bottomed, ovenproof pot and seal the portions on all sides. Add garlic cloves, cover and cook in the oven for 45 minutes or until the skin is crispy. Check the meat for tenderness with a skewer. If not serving immediately, set aside and allow to cool in fat, or chill, covered with the fat.

Combine all the ingredients for the noodle sauce.

Break the tagliatelle in half and cook in boiling water with oil but no salt. Strain and toss immediately in 60 ml of noodle sauce.

For the duck sauce, heat 10 ml duck fat and stir in the flour to make a roux. Add the orange juice and an equal quantity of duck stock and stir until smooth. Add the Triple Sec.

To assemble the dish, take one portion of duck per serving and scrape off the cold fat. Remove the meat from the bone and shred. Heat a little duck sauce in a small pan and quickly toss the meat in the sauce to warm through. Reheat the noodles in a small knob of butter warmed in a pan. Season with salt and ground pepper, and toss in the rest of the noodle sauce, with a few torn fresh mint and coriander leaves.

To serve, place noodles in the centre of the plate. Pile shredded duck on top of the noodles and garnish with a large sprig of fresh coriander.

serves 4

wine suggestion
Beyerskloof Pinotage

moroccan fish

The Burgundy
Restaurant, Hermanus

2 portions linefish
45 ml olive oil

paste
125 ml dried chilles,
stems removed
2 cloves garlic, peeled
15 ml coarse salt
15 ml ground cumin
7.5 ml ground coriander
30 ml olive oil

garnish
lemon wedges
fresh coriander

To make the paste, soak the chillies in hot water until soft. Pound the garlic with half of the salt until smooth. Remove from the mortar and grind chillies to a smooth paste with the remaining salt. Combine all the ingredients and blend well. This will keep indefinitely in a sealed jar in the refrigerator.

Spread some of the paste on the fish. Heat 15 ml olive oil in a pan. Add the fish, skin-side up and fry until half cooked. Turn the fish and fry on the other side. Place the fish on a plate garnished with lemon wedges and fresh coriander. Serve with rice and a fresh garden salad.

serves 2

wine suggestion
Theuniskraal Riesling

amarula truffles

marine fruit soufflé

amarula truffles

La Loerie, Knysna

Melt the chocolate in a bain marie, stir in the cream, sifted icing sugar, Amarula and vanilla essence and stir until quite smooth. Place the bowl with the chocolate mixture on a flat tray and chill in freezer for approximately 2 hours. Remove from freezer and roll into small balls, then coat them with the cocoa powder. Serve with a ball of ice cream and garnish with whipped cream. Pour a dash of Amarula over the cream and ice cream.

50 g dark chocolate
50 g milk chocolate
25 ml cream
50 ml icing sugar, sifted
20 ml Amarula Cream
    Liqueur
1 ml vanilla essence
cocoa powder
1 ball of vanilla ice cream
whipped cream for garnish
extra Amarula Cream
    Liqueur

serves 1

wine suggestion
Neethlingshof Noble Late Harvest

marine fruit soufflé

The Marine Hotel, Hermanus

Bring purée, sugar and lemon juice to the boil. Mix the cornflour with a little water and pour it slowly into the boiling liquid, whisking continuously. Remove from heat and cool. Whisk the egg whites until just peaking. Briskly whisk $1/3$ of the meringue into the fruit mixture, then very gently fold in the rest. Pipe into 8 buttered and sugared ramekins (double buttered: butter, sugar, butter). Level off and place a greased egg shell half in the centre of each to make a well during baking. Bake at 190 °C for 15–20 minutes – it will triple in size. Remove the egg shells and fill the hollows with melba sauce or fruit coulis.

200 g fruit purée
40 ml sugar
5 ml lemon juice
30 ml cornflour
water
4 egg whites
40 ml sugar for ramekins
30 ml butter for ramekins
    and egg shells
8 egg shell halves
melba sauce or fruit coulis

serves 8

wine suggestion
Dewetshof Estate Edeloes Noble Late Harvest

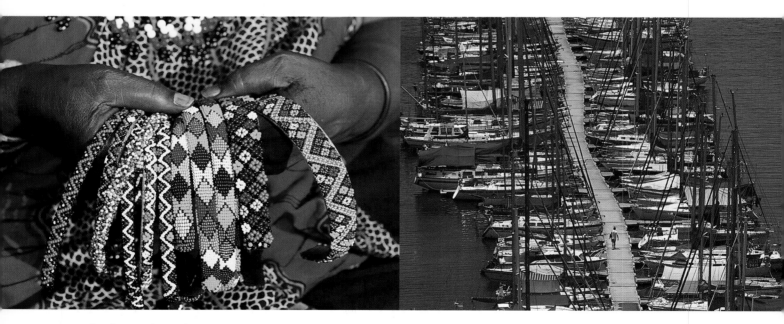

zulu beadwork

yacht basin, durban

kwazulu-natal

indian market, durban

margate

From its border with the Eastern Cape Province, the view for 200 kilometres up the southern KwaZulu-Natal coast is of one big holiday resort. At least 20 coastal towns lie one beside the other, creating a continuous subtropical playground of long, unbroken beaches, generous sunshine and warm water. And if other provinces look askance at its unabashed pursuit of fun in the sun, they would do well to note its impressive nature reserves and long history of conservation.

The resorts end abruptly about one-third up the coast, at Ballito, north of the major harbour city of Durban. From this point on, the shoreline and adjacent interior is almost entirely given up to magnificent parks, reserves and wilderness areas recognised internationally for their unique ecosystems and advanced conservation management. In this, South Africa's smallest province, more than 30 parks have emerged in the course of a hundred years of conservation. Two of the most important are the Hluhluwe-Umfolozi Park, where black and white rhinos have been saved from extinction in acclaimed conservation projects, and the Greater St Lucia Wetland Park, recently proclaimed a World Heritage Site.

Above: The Botshabelo Ndebele Cultural Village sells fine examples of local traditional arts and crafts in what was once a mission station.

Opposite: Durban's esplanade is a landmark in a city given over almost entirely to the gratification of holiday-makers. Should the beaches pall, there are many other attractions – playgrounds and open-air theatre, craft markets and the wonders of Sea World nearby, where visitors can view a host of ocean-dwellers.

The Greater St Lucia Wetland Park is acclaimed as one of the world's most significant wetland areas. It is a fragile composition of wetlands and estuaries, coastal and dune forests, mangrove swamps and savanna, with the shallow salt-water Lake St Lucia as its focal point. Pelicans at the Nsumu pan are among the many protected residents of the sanctuary.

Below: The Natal Drakensberg, bordering on the mountain kingdom of Lesotho, is one of the most scenic regions of the country. The highest peaks at Giant's Castle are part of the lovely Giant's Castle Game Reserve, which is said to contain almost half of all the rock art found in South Africa.

Right: The Tugela River in full spate after winter snows, in the Royal Natal National Park. The centre-piece of this magnificent park in the northern Drakensberg is the Amphitheatre, a natural rock feature lying between two buttresses.

In spite of its status as one of South Africa's principal ports and its fastest-growing city, Durban does not have the title of provincial capital. This belongs to Pietermaritzburg, a gracious town characterised by lavish Victorian architecture. About an hour's drive inland from Durban, Pietermaritzburg is elegant and orderly in its layout and justly boasts of its beautiful gardens and parks. Durban's architectural attractions are equally noteworthy but play second fiddle to surf, sand and a subtropical climate that attracts waves of sun-seekers throughout the year. The city's harbour handles more cargo than all other South African ports combined, including vast quantities of sugar from the surrounding fields. The sugarcane fields were established and worked with the help of indentured labour brought from India in the 19th century. Today, Durban's one-million strong Indian population is largely descended from these people who have contributed so richly to the culture, commercial, economic and agricultural growth, not to mention the cuisine of the country.

It's to be expected that Durban – indeed the whole of KwaZulu-Natal – is the place to go for Indian food representing every region of the faraway homelands. The Indian Market is a treasure-trove of brilliant spices, silks and brassware that is not to be missed by any enthusiastic shopper in search of serious 'retail therapy'.

Natal's history has been one of bloody conflict between Boer, Brit and the Zulu nation, much of it centred around the now-serene town of Eshowe. Nearby, Shakaland recreates the Zulu culture in a living open-air museum where traditional food – simple fare such as samp and beans, mieliepap, baked pumpkin and sweet potatoes – is served, and 'wardances' are merely for the gratification of tourists.

The beautiful Midlands area, en route to the Drakensberg and the Lesotho border, is a narrow passage of evergreen hills and valleys reminiscent of England's west country. Its lovely scenery is highlighted along the route known as the Midlands Meander, which weaves

Opposite: Resplendent in horned headdress and beaded, mirrored 'apron', a Durban beachfront rickshaw operator takes Zulu traditional dress into undreamt-of dimensions in order to attract business. Their costumes have become more elaborate over the years, while their numbers have dwindled – from almost 1 000 in the 1930s to less than 20 today.

Below: The Midlands Meander leads visitors through the most scenic countryside to the studios and galleries of resident artists, as well as fine restaurants and inns.

past craft shops and galleries, country lodges, and restaurants serving the exquisite trout that proliferate in the lakes and streams – and in the many commercial hatcheries – of the region. Local menus have a strong British flavour, featuring game birds, wild asparagus, mushrooms and berries freely found by the roadsides.

The Midlands is within easy reach of the spectacular Drakensberg, which create a natural barrier between Natal and its neighbours, the Free State and Lesotho. This is one of the most scenic regions of the country. Named the 'dragon mountains' by settlers, and 'spears' by the Zulu people, the eastern face of the Natal Drakensberg is an awesome composition of pinnacles, buttresses and natural amphitheatres that are an irresistible lure to those in search of union with nature. The Royal Natal National Park incorporates 8 000 hectares of the 'Berg's most breathtaking terrain. The centrepiece of this magnificent park in the northern Drakensberg is the Amphitheatre, a natural rock feature lying between two buttresses each over 3 000 metres high.

The highest peaks at Giant's Castle – which in winter are always covered in snow – are part of the lovely Giant's Castle Game Reserve, which is said to contain almost half of all the rock art found in South Africa. In spring when the snow begins to melt, waterfalls such as Jacob's Ladder Falls descend in measured succession through forested gorges in the Loteni Nature Reserve. The reserves and protected areas of state forest in the southern Drakensberg form a continuous green wilderness zone with unlimited walking, hiking and bird-watching opportunities for eco-conscious travellers, making this a nature lover's heaven.

Below The Greater St Lucia Wetland Park is one of South Africa's three recently named World Heritage sites, and acclaimed as one of the world's most significant wetland areas. It is a fragile composition of wetlands and estuaries, coastal and dune forests, mangrove swamps and savanna, with the shallow salt-water Lake St Lucia as its focal point. Pelicans at the Nsumu pan are among the many protected residents of the sanctuary.

snails in phyllo with cherry tomato relish

Granny Mouse Country
House, Old Main Road,
Balgowan

24 snails (if using tinned
   snails, strain off juices)
5 ml crushed garlic
pinch of finely chopped
   chives
1/4 onion, finely diced
butter and olive oil
   for frying
salt and freshly ground
   black pepper
squeeze of fresh lime
36 squares phyllo pastry,
   each 8 cm x 8 cm

cherry tomato relish
250 ml olive oil
1/2 punnet red cherry
   tomatoes
small handful yellow plum
   cherry tomatoes
2 sprigs fresh basil
1 sprig thyme
2 cloves garlic, peeled
pinch of salt
ground lemon pepper
5 ml pink peppercorns

Sauté snails, garlic, chives and onion in
butter and olive oil. Season with salt,
pepper and lime. Allow to cool.

Baste together 3 squares of phyllo
pastry. Place 2 snails and some sauce in
the centre and bring corners of pastry
together. Brush with olive oil and bake at
100 °C until slightly browned. Increase
heat if necessary to brown evenly.

For the relish, heat the olive oil until
hot, add all the remaining ingredients and
allow to simmer for a few minutes. It is
best done the day before and reheated
before use.

To serve, spoon warmed relish onto
a plate, and place phyllo parcel on top.

serves 4

wine suggestion
Pierre Jordaan Chameleon
Sauvignon Blanc

smoked mountain trout pasta

Thokozisa Mountain
Café, Route 600,
Central Drakensberg

Poach garlic in a small amount of cream
and then add all the lemon zest, lemon
juice, saffron and salt. Reduce liquid until
sauce thickens, then add trout broken
up into small pieces. Heat through for
2 minutes. Add precooked pasta, mixing
in the ground black pepper, chives and the
vodka. Serve garnished with lemon slices,
chives and fresh dill tips.

serves 2

wine suggestion
Saxenburg Grand Vin Blanc

5 ml crushed garlic
250 ml fresh cream
grated zest of ¼ lemon
juice of 1 lemon
pinch of saffron
salt to taste
1 whole smoked trout,
    filleted
200 g tagliatelle, cooked
    until al dente
freshly ground black
    pepper
garlic chives, chopped
1 tot vodka

garnish
lemon slices
chives
fresh dill tips

crayfish timbale

The Royal Grill, Royal Hotel, Durban

2 steamed crayfish tails,
   peeled and sliced
2 ripe avocados, peeled
   and diced
4 ripe tomatoes, peeled
   and diced
30 ml mascarpone cheese
30 ml dried dill
100 ml basic vinaigrette
100 ml balsamic vinegar

Oil the inside of a stainless-steel pipe, about 80 mm in diameter and 80 mm in height. Simply arrange the crayfish, avocado and tomato in layers in te pipe, repeating this arrangement twice and leaving about 10 mm free at the top. Spread the mascarpone cheese on top. Carefully remove the pipe.

Infuse the dill in the vinaigrette. Bring the balsamic vinegar to the boil and cook until reduced by half. Carefully arrange the timbale in the centre of a white plate and drizzle the vinaigrette around the one half of the plate, and the balsamic vinegar around the other half. Garnish with a large sprig of fresh dill.

serves 4

hot-and-sour spinach with honeyed sesame prawns

The Rainbow Terrace, Durban Hilton

To prepare the hot-and-sour spinach, heat the oil in a pan. Add beetroot, carrots, chillies and spinach. Toss over high heat, add Chinese noodles and mix well. Add vinegar, then soya sauce. Season to taste. Drain off excess liquid and keep warm.

To prepare batter, mix flour, salt and pepper. Add egg and water and beat thoroughly until smooth.

Season prawns with salt and pepper, toss in cornflour and shake off excess. Place prawns in batter and coat well.

Fry in heated oil until golden brown and drain on absorbent paper. Keep prawns warm. Mix sesame seed oil and honey and very gently heat through. Add sesame seeds. Keep warm.

To serve, place spinach mixture in centre of plate. Set 2 prawns on spinach and the third on top of the 2 prawns with tail facing upwards. Pour sesame and honey mixture over the prawns and serve garnished with a piece of fennel leaf.

serves 4

wine suggestion
Middelvlei Chardonnay 1998

hot-and-sour spinach
100 ml oil
2 medium uncooked
   beetroot, cubed
2 medium carrots, julienned
40 g chillies, finely chopped
500 g blanched spinach,
   excess water drained
100 g blanched Chinese
   noodles, e.g. glass
   noodles
50 ml red wine vinegar
100 ml soya sauce
salt and pepper to taste

batter
100 g self-raising flour
pinch of salt and pepper
1 lightly beaten egg
140 ml water

**honeyed sesame
   prawns**
12 queen-sized prawns,
   shelled and deveined,
   with tails on
30 ml salt
45 ml cornflour
oil for frying
100 ml sesame seed oil
40 ml honey
15 ml sesame seeds,
   toasted

garnish
fennel leaves

the royal chicken & prawn curry

The Royal Grill,
Royal Hotel,
Durban

150 ml clarified butter

1 medium onion, finely chopped

45 ml ginger paste

45 ml garlic paste

80 ml curry powder (mild or hot
according to preference)

10 ml turmeric

2 medium tomatoes, liquidised

800 g chicken breast, cut into strips

800 g queen prawns, cleaned and
deveined, tails left on

250 ml fresh cream

chopped fresh coriander

chopped fresh curry leaves

salt to taste

30 ml ground cumin

Heat a pan and add clarified butter. Add finely
chopped onion and sauté until transparent.
Add ginger and garlic paste, then curry powder,
turmeric and tomato. Cover and simmer for
5 minutes. Add the chicken strips and cook for
10 minutes. Add the prawns and cook 5 minutes,
then add cream and cook again for 5 minutes.
Add coriander and curry leaves and salt to taste.
Garnish with ground cumin, and serve with
basmati rice and a choice of pickles.

serves 5

warm pear and chocolate tart with almond sabayon

The Rainbow Terrace, Durban Hilton

sugar base dough
100 g butter
100 ml sugar
1 egg
310 ml cake flour
1 ml baking powder
1 ml salt

frangipani
100 ml castor sugar
125 g butter
2 eggs
125 g ground almonds
60 ml cake flour
30 ml cocoa
1 ml salt
1 ml vanilla essence
4 pears, peeled, cored
    and thinly sliced.

sabayon
2 egg yolks
125 ml sugar syrup
2 ml almond essence

to serve
toasted almonds
icing sugar
whipped cream
fresh mint leaves

For the sugar base dough, cream butter and sugar. Add eggs and incorporate well. Add flour, baking powder and salt and mix in well. On a floured surface, roll out the dough to about 5 mm thick. Lift into a 25 cm loose-bottomed tin. Press into the sides and trim the edges. Refrigerate.

For the frangipani, cream sugar and butter. Add eggs and mix well. Add the almonds, flour, cocoa, salt and vanilla. Mix well to combine all the ingredients. Spread half the mixture over the pastry base. Fan the pear over the mixture, then cover with remaining frangipani mixture. Bake at 180 °C for about 30 minutes until the frangipani is set.

For the sabayon, mix the egg yolks, sugar syrup and almond essence together in a double boiler. Whisk until the mixture is thick and creamy. The temperature should not be too high otherwise the sabayon will separate.

To serve, pour a pool of almond sabayon on each plate and place a slice of pear tart on top. Sprinkle with toasted almonds and dust with icing sugar. Serve with a spoon of whipped cream, decorated with a mint leaf.

serves 8

wine suggestion
Pierre Jordaan Ratafia

crème brûlée

The Royal Grill, Royal Hotel, Durban

Add the split vanilla pod to the cream and heat to just under boiling point. Allow to cool slightly. Whisk egg and sugar, then add the egg mixture to the cooled cream. Strain mixture then add dates. Pour the mixture into appropriate dishes and bake in a bain-marie at 150 °C for about 10 minutes until set. Cool and refrigerate. Sprinkle with castor sugar and gratinate under the salamander to form a sugar crust. Serve with cinnamon ice cream and garnish with fresh mint leaves.

serves 10, depending on size of dishes used

1 vanilla pod
1 litre fresh cream
10 egg yolks
150 ml white sugar
250 g pitted dates,
    chopped
castor sugar

to serve
cinnamon ice cream
fresh mint leaves

fresh mountain blueberry cheesecake

Thokozisa Mountain
Café, Route 600,
Central Drakensberg

Crush the biscuits and blend with melted butter.
Mould the mixture into the base of a 24 cm loose-
bottomed, expandable cake tin. Dissolve jelly in
water and mix in sugar. Now fold in the fresh cream
and cottage cheese. Pour into the mould and allow
to set until firm.

For the blueberry topping, pulp the berries
and add sugar and wine. Gently stir over a low
heat, adding a little water if necessary to produce
a paste consistency.

To serve, spread a thin layer of blueberry
topping over the top of the cheesecake and
garnish with sprigs of fresh mint.

serves 8

1 packet tennis biscuits
180 ml melted butter
250 ml lemon jelly powder
250 ml boiling water
180 ml castor sugar
500 ml fresh cream
500 ml creamed cottage
  cheese

blueberry topping
1 punnet fresh blueberries
125 ml castor sugar
125 ml red wine

garnish
fresh mint

traditional dwellings

free state plateau

free state

cosmos

maluti mountains

The Free State occupies the high, sunny uplands of South Africa, bordered by the mountain kingdom of Lesotho in the east and two major rivers, the Orange in the south and the Vaal in the north. Its rich plains support a thriving agriculturally based economy underpinned by the wealth from mining diamonds, gold and uranium.

It is a generous land, with kind and hospitable people who live close to the earth and readily share its bounty. The Free State produces huge quantities of maize, beef, mutton, wool, wheat, sunflowers, groundnuts, vegetables including a major percentage of the nation's store of potatoes and pumpkins, and luxury crops such as asparagus and cherries. Game, particularly the endemic blesbok, is plentiful, and features prominently on seasonal menus. Teamed with the superb local produce and washed down with delicious and nicely alcoholic berry, cherry and plum wines, it is a meal approaching celestial heights.

Laden with history and lined with fine Victorian buildings of golden-hued sandstone, the small towns of the sunny Free State are repositories for Anglo-Boer war relics, San artefacts, museums and mission churches, blockhouses and battlesites, and in Harrismith, a 150-million-year-old petrified tree, *Dadoxylon solerosum*. At Koffiefontein, known for its open diamond mines, Italian prisoners of war and sympathisers were interned during the Second World War, and a mural depicting Mussolini still stands in the memorial garden. Not far from Harrismith, the Platberg is home to the Drakensberg and Free State Botanic Garden.

Above: Late afternoon clouds on the Free State landscape usually presage a brief but welcome thunderstorm that refreshes the red earth and supplies life-giving moisture to animals and crops.

Opposite: Fields of sunflowers turn their faces to the sun on farmlands near Kroonstad. Agriculture and its by-products – vegetable oils, dairy products, beef and maize – are the mainstay of the Free State's economy.

The region has had as many names as changes of ownership. It was first the preserve of the San people, who have left reminders of their centuries-long presence in delicate rock art and other artefacts throughout the Free State. The earliest name was derived from the Khoikhoi title for the Gariep (great river) at its southern edge, and it was known as Transgariep. It changed hands between Boer and Brit until after the 1994 elections, when the small province finally gained its titular 'liberty' and became the Free State.

Its history, embodied in the beautiful provincial capital of Bloemfontein, was summed up by British author Anthony Trollope in the 1870s: 'This is a place that has been fought for by many, lost by some, and won by others who saw in it something too rich to give up.'

Bloemfontein, the City of Roses and judicial capital of South Africa, was a pivotal supply and communications centre during the Anglo-Boer War. The Women's Monument in the town is a poignant reminder of the more than 26 000 women and children who died during the war.

Below: *The Free State's Golden Gate Highlands National Park is entered through a massive cleft in the sandstone Rooiberg range. Monumental rock 'sculptures' such as this are a signature of the park's unforgettable landscapes.*

Although a landlocked province, the Free State has plenty to offer by way of watersports and fishing at the resorts and nature reserves along the Vaal River. Two lovely reserves are within easy reach of Bloemfontein, one on the south and the other on the north shore of the Vaal. The Sandveld Nature Reserve hosts abundant waterfowl on its sandflats, while the adjoining Bloemhof Dam – the fifth largest in the country – provides a waterside retreat in the summer heat. The popular Rob Ferreira resort west of the town of Bloemhof has curative hot springs on the doorstep of a reserve well-stocked with antelope, zebra and a small number of white rhino.

The focal point of the eastern Free State is the serenely beautiful Golden Gate Highlands National Park, which encompasses magnificent scenery from the highest plateau in South Africa. The portals that give the park its name are twin sandstone massifs cleft in the Rooiberg range by the passage, over many millennia, of the Little Caledon River.

Below: The Platberg – or flat-topped mountain – near Harrismith was once the site of a British base during the Anglo-Boer War, with a National Monument blockhouse as a reminder. Another curiousity is a petrified tree, thought to be 150 million years old, in the town centre.

butternut, crab and lemon grass soup

Cranberry Cottage,
Ladybrand, Free State

1 kg butternut, peeled
  and cubed
2 cloves garlic, crushed
2 litres hot chicken stock
30 ml butter
60 ml flour
10 ml medium curry
  powder
2 ml chilli powder
2 stalks fresh lemon grass,
  chopped
20 ml dried coriander
  leaves
425 g tin coconut milk
170 g tin crab meat
10 ml soya sauce
salt and white pepper
lemon juice to taste
125 ml cream

Steam the butternut and garlic until soft, remove from steamer and purée together with some of the chicken stock until smooth. Heat the butter in a saucepan and add the flour to make a roux. Add the curry powder, chilli powder, lemon grass and half the coriander, and stir well for a minute. Pour in the remainde of the hot chicken stock and bring to the boil. Boil until smooth and thickened, then stir in the puréed butternut. Cook for 5 minutes to combine the flavours. Add the coconut milk, crab meat (including the juice) and soya sauce and season to taste with salt, pepper and a dash of lemon juice. To serve, stir in a swirl of cream.

serves 6–8

wine suggestion
Louisvale Chavant

sunnybrae farmhouse soup

Maluti Mountain Lodge,
Clarens, Free State

30 ml butter
15 ml crushed garlic
125 ml olive oil
5 onions, chopped
2 slices beef shin
6 marrow bones
4 leeks, sliced
1 bunch celery, sliced
2 turnips, chopped
3 x 800 g tins whole peeled
    tomatoes
2 x 410 g tins Italian Barloti
    beans or small white
    beans
500 ml barley
6 litres beef stock
250 ml pasta shells
125 ml chopped fresh
    mixed herbs
salt and pepper to taste
15 ml basil pesto
Parmesan cheese

Heat butter, garlic and olive oil in a large pot. Fry the onions until soft and brown. Add the chopped shin meat and marrow bones, vegetables, beans, barley and stock. Cook slowly for 3 hours, then add the pasta shells, herbs, salt and pepper to taste, and lastly the pesto. When the pasta shells are al dente, serve with a generous sprinkle of Parmesan cheese.

serves 25

roasted duck, cherry and port pie

Maluti Mountain Lodge,
Clarens, Free State

Clean the duck thoroughly. Brush with melted butter and season liberally with salt and pepper. Prick skin all over with a fork. Place on a rack over a roasting pan in a preheated oven at 200 °C for 1½ hours, turning occasionally. Cool, then remove meat and dice into bite-sized pieces.

For the sauce, melt the butter, add the drained cherries and heat through. Pour in brandy and light. Stir in redcurrant jelly, orange juice and rind. Add stock and reserved cherry juice. Season to taste. Blend cornflour and water and stir into sauce. Bring to the boil, stirring constantly, until sauce thickens. Add duck meat and allow to cool.

Place duck and sauce in five au gratin dishes. Roll out pastry and cut into narrow strips for lattice. Arrange pastry in a lattice pattern over duck and make cut-outs to line the edge of the dish. Brush with egg and bake at 220 °C for 20–25 minutes until pastry has puffed and is golden brown.

Makes 5 pies

wine suggestion
Neil Ellis Cabernet/Merlot Blend

1 x 2 kg duck
25 ml melted butter
salt and pepper

sauce
25 ml butter
410 g tin black cherries, pitted and drained, juice reserved
25 ml brandy
25 ml redcurrant jelly
juice and finely grated rind of 1 orange
125 ml chicken stock
75 ml reserved cherry juice
salt and pepper
25 ml cornflour
15 ml water

pastry lattice
200 g puff pastry
1 egg, lightly beaten

roast knuckle of spring lamb

Cranberry Cottage,
Ladybrand, Free State

6 x 500 g lamb knuckles
   cut high on the leg
60 ml flour
5 ml mixed spice
salt and pepper
10 ml crushed garlic
zest of 2 lemons
5 ml dried rosemary
250 ml beef stock
75 ml dry white wine

Dust knuckles with 30 ml of the flour, spices, salt and pepper
and sprinkle with the garlic. Place in an oven bag with the
remaining flour, lemon zest, rosemary, beef stock and white
wine. Place in a baking dish, prick the oven bag twice on the
upper side, and cook at 180 °C for 1 hour until pink. Slice
open the bag and remove knuckles, placing one knuckle on
each plate. Pour over gravy from meat and serve with mashed
potato and fresh vegetables.

serves 6

toasted hazelnut icebox

Cranberry Cottage, Ladybrand, Free State

12 egg yolks
175 ml golden syrup
30 ml coffee liqueur
30 ml instant coffee
    granules
175 g plain chocolate
    broken into pieces
750 ml double or whipping
    cream

garnish
hazelnut praline
toasted hazelnuts

Using an electric mixer, beat the egg yolks and golden syrup together in a large mixing bowl for about 4 minutes until slightly thickened and pale. Pour the egg yolk mixture into a large non-stick saucepan. Cook for approximately 30 minutes over low heat, stirring constantly, until the mixture thickens and coats a spoon well. Remove from heat. Pour two-thirds of the egg yolk mixture into a large bowl. In a cup, stir the coffee liqueur and coffee granules together, stir into the egg yolk mixture in the large bowl. In a bowl over a pan of gently simmering water, heat half of the chocolate, stirring frequently, until melted and smooth. Stir the melted chocolate into the remaining egg yolk mixture in the saucepan until blended.

In another large bowl, whip 600 ml of the double or whipping cream until soft peaks form. With a rubber spatula or wire whisk, fold two-thirds of the whipped cream into the coffee mixture until blended. Fold the remaining whipped cream into the chocolate mixture.

Spoon half of the coffee mixture into a 23 cm springform cake tin, spreading evenly, and freeze until set – about 15 minutes. Remove the tin from the refrigerator and spread the chocolate mixture evenly over the coffee layer, and again freeze until set – about 15 minutes.

Sprinkle the chocolate layer with hazelnut praline, and top with the remaining coffee mixture. Cover and freeze until firm – at least 4 hours.

In a bowl over a pan of gently simmering water, heat the remaining chocolate, stirring often, until melted and smooth. Remove the saucepan from the heat. Cut non-stick baking parchment into two 10 cm squares. Moisten a large baking sheet with water. Place parchment squares on the baking sheet (water will prevent the paper from slipping). Spoon melted chocolate onto the squares and shape into triangles. Refrigerate.

In a small bowl, whip remaining double or whipping cream until stiff peaks form. Spoon whipped cream into a piping bag fitted with a star tube. Run the blade of a palette knife dipped in hot water around the edge of the springform tin to loosen the cake, and remove the side of the tin.

Pipe whipped cream into 8 flowers around the edge of the cake. Place chocolate triangles between the whipped cream flowers. Decorate with toasted hazelnuts. Leave cake at room temperature for about 5 minutes for easier slicing.

serves 10

wine suggestion
Graham Beck Rhona Muscadel

raspberry cheesecake with a raspberry vodka coulis

Maluti Mountain Lodge, Clarens, Free State

Whip the cream until thick then mix all the ingredients except the biscuits and butter together and stir until smooth. Crush the biscuits, mix with melted butter and push into the bottom of a serving dish. Pour the cheesecake mixture into the dish and refrigerate to set. Lay fresh raspberries on top, and serve with coulis and a fresh mint leaf for garnish.

For the coulis, mix all the ingredients in a blender until smooth.

serves 12

750 ml fresh cream
250 ml fresh raspberries, crushed
500 ml smooth cream cheese
2 tins condensed milk
25 ml gelatine
1 packet tennis biscuits
1 packet shortbread biscuits
30 ml butter, melted

coulis
250 ml fresh raspberries
15 ml castor sugar
250 ml water
2 tots vodka

garnish
fresh raspberries
mint leaves

tea pickers

pretoria

gauteng
northern province
& north-west

zulu dancers

gold reef city

Above: *A timid impala* (Aepyceros melampus)*, ever wary of predators, takes a tentative turn at a Kruger National Park water hole.*

The immense spaces of this region at the northern extremity of South Africa contain some of the country's most dramatic contrasts. Even more intriguing than the lure of the coast and its commercial playgrounds is the notion that wild animals roam in the beautiful Kruger National Park a few hours north of Johannesburg – and that not far from Pretoria in the awesome surrounds of the Sterkfontein caves (a World Heritage Site), man may look into the face of his origins in the form of Mrs Ples, the first adult skull of *Australopithecus africanus transvaalensis*, discovered by Dr Robert Broom in 1936. Or that it is possible to explore a fossilised cycad forest – home of the rain queen that inspired Rider Haggard's famous novel *She* – a morning's drive from one of the biggest adult theme parks in the world, the glittering Vegas-style Sun City Resort and Casino Complex, near the rim of an extinct volcano.

Johannesburg, the metropolis at the heart of the region, may have been no more than a sprawl of farmland today if it had not been for the discovery of a gold-bearing reef on the farm Langlaagte in 1886, which precipitated the biggest gold rush in history. Egoli – The City of Gold – is a pivotal entry point for travellers to all parts of Africa, and a major player in international finance, engineering and manufacturing. It is both chic and shabby, beautiful and, in parts, ugly, but for six million people, Jo'burg is home.

Opposite: *The majestic cheetah* (Acinonyx jubatus). *Luxurious private reserves offer visitors personalised safaris and game-viewing with private rangers.*

Pretoria, 56 kilometres north of Johannesburg, is the country's administrative and diplomatic capital.

Previous pages: *A fabulous man-made*
'kingdom' of magical lakes, mystical
forests and a 'palace of the lost city'
has risen from the barren landscapes
of the North-West Province. The Sun
City Resort and Casino complex has
created recreational – and employment
– opportunities for the province.

Above: *The Hartbeespoort Dam*
at the midpoint of the Magaliesberg
range provides northerners with a great
holiday destination with more reliable
weather than the beaches of the
southern Cape.

Elegantly laid out at the eastern foothills of the Magaliesberg, Pretoria is famed for its jacaranda trees, which cast a lilac mantle over the city in spring and summer. The ancient Magaliesberg range spans 160 kilometres between Pretoria and the beautiful town of Rustenberg to the west, and was once the preserve of stone- and iron-age man – and 'Mrs Ples' – who inhabited the abundantly wooded kloofs, gathering water from the falls and streams and living well off the game of a 'landscape covered with elephants'.

The many beautiful spots in the Magaliesberg, including the resorts around the Hartbeespoort Dam provide a host of holiday destinations every bit as enjoyable, and with more reliable weather, than the celebrated beaches on the southern Cape coast. The Dam provides wonderful opportunities for a host of watersports, and is a favourite destination for yachtsmen as permanent berthing facilties are available here.

The Pilanesberg Game Park bordering Sun City is a model reserve that has, in the last 30 years, recovered a near-complete assembly of the original fauna in an acclaimed game-stocking project coined 'Operation Genesis'.

The region's rich history has entangled people of many nations, and many tribes. There are forts and blockhouses left by Boer and Brit after the turn-of-the-century war, and museums that record the victories and defeats of men embattled in the pursuit of gold. The infamous Jameson Raid was launched from the British fort at Kanonkop, outside the North West capital city of Mafikeng. And it was here that Colonel Robert Baden-Powell, founder of the Boy Scout movement, headed the British garrision that defended the town until the celebrated 'Relief of Mafeking'. Today's Mafikeng is a peaceful place where beef and dairy are produced on a massive scale.

Above: The Union buildings, designed by Sir Herbert Baker, bask in the glow of a million jacaranda blossoms that throw a purple mantle over the city of Pretoria in the spring and summer months.

But for many visitors, it will be the life of the present residents, whose ancestors owned the land long before European intervention, that is most arresting. The traditions and customs of the early people – Ndbele, Batswana, Bushman, Zulu, Xhosa and VhaVenda – are carefully preserved in cultural villages such as Lesedi and Moruleng. Visitors can enjoy traditional food and accommodation, and have a sangoma throw the bones.

The mystical VhaVenda people occupy the Letaba Valley east of Pietersburg, a subtropical paradise at the gateway to the mist-shrouded indigenous forests and waterfalls of the Magoebaskloof. Important Venda mythology sites can be seen at Thathe Vondo Sacred Forest, and at Lake Fundudzi, sacred home of the python god, which may be visited only with permission of the priestess of the lake. The largest baobab in Africa stands at the ruins of the Tshiungane stone fortifications, near Sagole; the baobab or cream of tartar tree can be used for its wood, pollen, leaves, seeds, fruit and pods.

Below: The city of Johannesburg is the second largest on the African continent, superseded only by Cairo.
It is home to 6 million people.

Opposite: The sun sets over Hillbrow, Johannesburg, an inner-city suburb of apartment blocks, restaurants, nightclubs and a seething population of residents from every country on earth.

At least half of the Kruger National Park's 20 000km² falls within the Northern Province, on its eastern frontier with Mozambique. These remote northern reaches are the meeting place of nine major ecosystems, which support a countless variety of animals, reptiles and insects. The mixed mopane scrub and forest is an ideal habitat for elephant, birds, rare roan antelope, tiny bushbuck and nyala – as well as crunchy mopane worms, prepared by roasting over an open fire. This is one of South Africa's main tourist attractions, and a favourite holiday destination.

snoek tart

Gramadoelas
Restaurant, Gauteng

quick puff pastry
500 g cake flour
5 ml cream of tartar
500 g butter
200 ml soda water
2 tots brandy

filling
250 ml white sauce
1 kg smoked snoek,
  deboned and flaked
2 medium onions, finely
  chopped and browned
  in a little oil
125 ml grated mature
  cheddar cheese

For the quick puff pastry, sift the flour and cream of tartar into a mixing bowl. Grate the butter and work it into the flour mixture with your fingers. Combine the soda water and brandy and mix it into the flour mixture. Let the dough rest overnight in the refrigerator. Allow it to soften at room temperature before rolling out onto a floured board until it is about 0.5 cm thick. Fold the pastry and refrigerate for 20 minutes before rolling out again as above. Bake blind and set aside.

To bake the pie shell 'blind', grease a pie dish with butter. Line the pie dish with pastry and press it into shape. Form a frill by pinching the pastry together around the edges. Fill the pie with dried beans – this prevents the pastry from rising in the centre, and helps keep the crust in shape. Bake at 200 °C for about 10–15 minutes. Cool and remove the beans.

Preheat the oven to 180 °C. First line the pastry shell with a little white sauce. Then add the flaked snoek and onion. Repeat once more, ending with a layer of white sauce. Cover with the grated cheese, then bake for 20 minutes or until the cheese is golden and bubbling.

serves 8

wine suggestion
Dewetshof Finesse Chardonnay

asparagus candy with langoustine ragoût

For the pasta dough, make a well in the flour, add the eggs, oil and salt, and rub in with fingertips. As soon as the mixture starts to bind, work it with the heel of the hand until smooth and elastic. Let it rest, covered with cling film.

For the asparagus filling, peel the end of the asparagus and cut off the tips, which are to be used as garnish. In a small saucepan, braise the shallot and garlic. Add the chopped asparagus and season to taste. Let the asparagus braise for 20 minutes over low heat, then set aside to cool. Add the ricotta and Parmesan. Cover with cling film and refrigerate.

For the langoustine ragoût, dice the langoustine tails and season with salt and pepper. Heat a little oil in a frying-pan, add the shallot and garlic and sauté for a couple of minutes. Add the tomato concasse, parsley, basil, and butter. Add the langoustine, then set aside.

For the asparagus candy, roll out a thin sheet of pasta dough, and cut it into 10 cm squares. Pipe in the asparagus filling, moisten the edges with a little water and roll up into a tube. Press and turn the edges to make candy-shaped pastas. Cook the candies for about 4 minutes in salted boiling water, then drain.

Serve on hot ragoût, garnished with parsley and blanched asparagus tips.

serves 4

wine suggestion
Boschendal Pongracz

Villa del Palazzo, Palace of the Lost City

pasta dough
500 ml cake flour
2 eggs
20 ml extra virgin olive oil
5 ml salt

asparagus filling
200 g fresh asparagus
1 small shallot, chopped
1/2 clove garlic, crushed
salt and pepper
200 g ricotta cheese
30 g Parmesan cheese

langoustine ragoût
300 g langoustine tails,
    cooked and peeled
salt and pepper
30 ml extra virgin olive oil
1/2 clove garlic, crushed
1/2 shallot, chopped
200 g tomato concasse
1 small bunch parsley,
    chopped
3 basil leaves, chopped
50 g unsalted butter

garnish
sprigs of parsley
blanched asparagus tips

mock leg of venison

Gramadoelas
Restaurant, Gauteng

250 ml red wine
10 ml sugar
1 ml ground ginger
6 whole cloves
6 rashers rindless bacon,
    cut into 1 cm strips
1 large onion, peeled and
    cut into rings
3 kg leg of lamb with all the
    fat trimmed off, but with
    the fell (parchment-like
    covering) left on
125 ml seedless raisins
4 garlic cloves, chopped
30 ml vegetable oil
10 ml salt
2 ml freshly ground black
    pepper
500 ml boiling water

sauce
30 ml apricot jam
15 ml cornflour
125 ml cold water

Starting a day ahead, combine the wine, sugar, ginger and cloves in a deep bowl and stir until the sugar and ginger are completely dissolved. Drop in the bacon strips and onion rings and turn them with a spoon until they are well coated. Marinate at room temperature for 15 minutes.

Remove the bacon from the marinade and lard the lamb. Using a small sharp knife, cut slits about 2 cm long and 3 cm deep on all sides of the leg of lamb, spacing the slits about 3 cm apart. Insert two or three raisins, garlic and a bacon strip into each slit. With the fingers, rub first the oil and then the salt and pepper all over the surface of the meat.

Place the lamb in an oven pan large enough to hold it comfortably and pour the marinade and onion rings over it. Cover the pan with foil and marinate the lamb at room temperature for several hours or overnight in the refrigerator.

Preheat the oven to 210 °C. Remove the leg of lamb from the marinade and place it on a wire rack over a grilling tray. Place the remaining marinade in the bottom of the tray and roast the leg for about 15 minutes to seal the meat.

Turn the heat down to 180 °C and roast for a further 1–1$^{1}/_{4}$ hours. Pour 500 ml boiling water into the bottom of the tray, if necessary, to prevent it from going dry.

Transfer the leg to a heated platter and place it in the warming oven.

To prepare the sauce, skim as much fat as possible from the liquid remaining in the pan and discard the cloves. Bring the liquid to the boil over a high heat. Cook briskly until the liquid has reduced to about 500 ml. Stir in the apricot jam and turn the heat down to low. Dissolve the cornflour in the cold water and stir it gradually into the simmering liquid. Cook, stirring frequently, for a few minutes until the sauce thickens. Taste for seasoning.

Mock leg of venison may be accompanied by separate bowls of potatoes, red cabbage cooked with quince or apples, and pickled yellow cling peaches.

serves 6–8

wine suggestion
Backsberg Klein Babylonstoren
Cabernet Merlot

grilled red snapper with braised mixed salad and tomato vinaigrette

Villa del Palazzo, Palace
of the Lost City

2 x 200 g red snapper fillets
2 medium tomatoes
5 basil leaves
5 ml salt
3 ml white pepper
20 ml balsamic vinegar
30 ml extra virgin olive oil
15 ml oil for braising
1 garlic clove, chopped
200 g mixed salad greens

Cut the fillets in half and make a few incisions in the skin. Peel the tomatoes and reserve the flesh for garnishing, and the core to make the tomato vinaigrette.

Put the core of the tomato in a blender and purée. Put through a sieve and return to blender with a couple of basil leaves, salt, pepper and balsamic vinegar. Blend the mixture, adding the oil little by little until the vinaigrette is smooth and thick.

Grill the fillet and set aside. Into a hot frying pan add oil, chopped garlic and mixed salad greens. Braise for a minute to just tenderise the salad, then add some of the diced tomato and chopped basil leaves, reserving some for the garnish.

To serve, place the salad in the middle of the plate, place the red snapper on top and season with vinaigrette. Garnish with reserved tomato and basil.

Serves 2

wine suggestion
Vergelegen Chardonnay

red roman fillets

Chagall's Restaurant,
Pretoria

tapenade
200 g dried black pitted
  olives
2 cloves garlic, peeled
  and chopped
2 anchovy fillets
50 ml olive oil
fresh thyme
2 large pinches freshly
  ground black pepper

spinach bed
4 bunches young Chinese
  spinach
1 small onion, chopped
  finely
15 ml butter
25 ml pastis

fish
8 red roman filets, fresh not
  frozen, deboned
3 litres water with leek,
  carrot, parsley, onion,
  peppercorns and salt

vinaigrette
200 ml extra virgin olive oil
100 ml raspberry vinegar
1 small onion, chopped
3 ripe tomatoes, seeded
  and cubed
freshly ground black
  pepper

For the tapenade, purée all the ingredients to a paste in a blender.

For the spinach bed, blanch the spinach in salted water, strain, squeeze dry and set aside. Sweat the onion in butter until golden. Add spinach, pastis and seasoning. Set aside and keep warm.

For the fish, bring the water and vegetables to a simmer. Add the fish filets and poach gently until nearly done. Remove and dry on absorbent paper.

For the vinaigrette, warm the olive oil very gently, add vinegar, brunoise onion and tomato and season with black pepper.

To serve, place spinach in the centre of the plate and top with the poached fillet. Spoon warm vinaigrette over the fish and round the spinach. Garnish with three tapenade quenelles (egg-shaped mounds of tapenade formed by pressing the paste between two teaspoons).

serves 4

wine suggestion
Riebeeck-Kasteel Tinta Barrocca Blend

grand marnier soufflé

Chagall's Restaurant,
Pretoria

Grease 6 small soufflé bowls with the butter and dust with castor sugar.

Warm the crème patisserie in a saucepan and add the egg yolks and Grand Marnier. Whisk until smooth and keep warm. Meanwhile beat the egg whites to a soft peak at medium speed, then add the castor sugar and lemon juice. This will help prevent separation from the whites. Increase the beater speed and beat the whites until firm but not too stiff. If too stiff, you will lose the texture and the soufflé will be too firm.

Now whisk about 1/4 of the beaten egg whites into the warm pastry cream until smooth. Gently fold in the remaining egg whites. Do not over mix or the soufflé will not rise. Fill the prepared soufflé bowls to the top, making sure the edges remain clean (this encourages even rising). If the soufflés do not rise evenly, use a sharp knife to free the edges where they are sticking to the bowl.

Bake for 10–15 minutes in a preheated oven at 200 °C. Remove the cooked soufflés from the oven, and serve immediately. The ideal soufflé should have a melting texture with a centre that is only just cooked. If undercooked, the soufflé will collapse.

Note: For extra orange flavour a mixture of boiled orange rind finely cubed and marinated in brandy could be added to the crème patisserie mixture.

serves 6

wine suggestion
Graham Beck Rhona

30 ml butter
30 ml castor sugar
200 ml crème patisserie
2 egg yolks
30 ml Grand Marnier
8 egg whites
60 ml castor sugar
5 ml lemon juice
icing sugar for dusting

tiramisú

Villa del Palazzo, Palace
of the Lost City

4 egg yolks
125 ml sugar
250 g mascarpone cheese
50 ml marsala wine
125 ml cream, whipped
1 plain sponge cake
500 ml espresso coffee
100 ml cocoa powder

Beat eggs and sugar until very stiff. Add a little of the mascarpone at a time while beating. Add marsala and keep on beating, then fold in the whipped cream. Let it rest for a while.

Moisten thin slices of sponge cake with coffee and line a mould. Add some cream mixture and cover with more sponge, repeating these steps until all the ingredients are finished. Chill for 2 hours, then dust with cocoa powder and serve.

serves 8

wine suggestion
Nederburg Edelkeur

zucchini cake

Gramadoelas
Restaurant, Gauteng

500 g baby marrow, grated
250 ml vegetable oil
375 ml sugar
3 eggs, well beaten
625 ml cake flour
7.5 ml baking powder
5 ml bicarbonate of soda
7.5 ml ground cinnamon
5 ml grated nutmeg
5 ml salt
250 ml pecan nuts

Heat the oven to 180 °C. Butter 1 large or 2 small loaf tins. Using a large mixing bowl, combine the baby marrow, oil, sugar and eggs. Sift the flour, baking powder, bicarbonate of soda, cinnamon, nutmeg and salt into the bowl and stir gradually until the ingredients are well mixed. Add the nuts and mix again. Spoon the mixture into the baking tin and bake on the middle rack of the oven for 1¼ hours. Test with a skewer – it should come out clean when the cake is ready. Remove the cake from the oven and allow to cool for 15 minutes before inverting it onto a wire rack. Allow to cool before serving.

serves 10

wine suggestion
Vin de Constance, the wine Napoleon requested on his deathbed, and which has now been reproduced by the Jooste family of Klein Constantia Estate.

zucchini cake   tiramisù

kruger national park

lisbon falls, graskop

mpumalanga

baobab tree

sabie river

Mpumalanga province covers almost 80 000 square kilometres of breathtaking terrain in the northern and eastern parts of South Africa. The high-lying interior plateau rises gradually from the west before plummeting over the rugged face of the 1 500 metre Escarpment to the Lowveld in the east, domain of the world-renowned Kruger National Park.

Unmistakably African, undeniably romantic, the region is alive with the history of big-game hunters and explorers, missionaries and fortune-seekers who were the first Europeans to probe the mysterious interior of the dark continent.

The Escarpment forms part of the spectacular northern Drakensberg – a place of waterfalls and forests, deep gorges and canyons, dark, quiet pools and trout-filled rivers. In contrast to the hot, dry bushveld below, the Escarpment is laden with moisture driven from the Indian Ocean which supports vast forests of eucalyptus and pine, fruit orchards, flowers and ferns.

The 22 500 hectare Blyde River Canyon Nature Reserve ranks with the Kruger Park as the pride of Mpumalanga. The 30-kilometre-long canyon is the centrepiece of the reserve, which has at its southern tip, one of the most beautiful views in South Africa – the appropriately named God's Window which 'opens' through a massive cut in the Escarpment. The majestic Canyon and its surrounds will keep visitors engrossed for days, exploring the pools and falls, caves and passes and small towns, beautifully preserved and brimming with history.

Above: A hopeful gold prospector named Tom Bourke gave his name to the potholes at the meeting place of the Treur and Blyde rivers in the reserve. The deep cylindrical potholes mark the start of the Blyde River's passage through the canyon.

Opposite: The 23 000 hectare Blyde River Canyon Nature Reserve encompasses some of the most remarkable scenery in southern Africa. The reserve is best explored on foot via a series of hiking trails and walks of varying intensity.

The circular Panorama Route maps out the highlights from the forested surrounds of Sabie via the spectacular Mac Mac, Berlin and Lisbon falls, to Bourke's Luck, where extraordinary potholes have been sculpted out of rock by aeons of rushing water and stones.

The route skirts the western boundary of the Blyde River reserve and continues past the Echo Caves, the historic Voortrekker town of Ohrigstad – once a mini-republic – and the old stone-walled Voortrekker entrenchment nearby, over Robbers' Pass to the national monument town of Pilgrim's Rest, a perfectly preserved example of a 19th-century mining town.

The Kruger National Park runs 350 kilometres from north to south along the eastern boundaries of both the Northern Province and Mpumalanga, giving each region roughly half of the cachet of ownership of one of the world's most famous wildlife sanctuaries. The

Above: *Gold was mined in Pilgrim's Rest for almost 100 years, the last mine closing in 1971. The small town has been restored and proclaimed a National Monument to preserve its rich historical record.*

Right: *The Botshabelo Cultural Village near Middelburg is a living museum of Ndebele craft and culture. Women's dress is heavily ornamental, conveying subtle messages through the use of colour and pattern.*

southern region features open savanna and densely wooded terrain bisected by several rivers which contribute to an array of specialised habitats for a wonderful diversity of flora and fauna. The Kruger Park accommodates the richest concentration of wildlife in the world in its two million hectares of African wilderness, and justifiably enjoys status as one of the great game parks on the continent. The Park offers superb accommodation as well as restaurant facilities. Although it is one of the main tourist attractions, it is also visited by South African families, who for generations have regarded this as one of their most popular holiday destinations.

Both in the Park and throughout the towns and reserves of Mpumalanga, there is an enormous choice of food and shelter for the traveller. He can indulge any whim, from five-star luxury in international hotels, elegant safari lodges and

exclusive country inns, right down to bush basics with a sleeping bag under the stars. Cuisine spans the entire spectrum from authentically African fare to menus indistinguishable from those in the restaurants of the culinary capitals of the world.

Everything is available – especially fresh seafood from Mozambique, KwaZulu-Natal and the Western Cape. Leading hotels and restaurants in the north have been known to charter their own fishing boats in Cape Town's Kalk Bay harbour to ensure a fresh daily supply – much to the chagrin of Capetonian restaurateurs accustomed to unlimited access to the daily haul.

The world's airlines bring imported delicacies – cheese, Champagne, caviar – to South African restaurant tables overnight. But in a region lavishly blessed with its own resources – exquisite trout, top-grade beef, various nuts, export-quality fresh fruit, and almost every vegetable under the sun – why sit down to foreign fare when you can eat what's grown on the doorstep, and dine like a king.

Opposite top: *The chacma baboon (Papio ursinus), the biggest member of the baboon species, is found throughout southern Africa.*

Opposite bottom: *Leopard (Panthera pardus) are among the most dangerous of predatory animals, and are counted as members of the Big Five.*

Bottom: *The Cape Buffalo (Syncerus caffer), also one of the Big Five, is known to be extremely dangerous when wounded. It is frequently predated by lion.*

critchley's beer bread

Critchley Hackle Lodge, Dullstroom, Mpumalanga

1.5 kg cake flour
1.5 kg Nutty Wheat flour
10 ml salt
250 ml brown sugar
250 g butter
3 x 340 ml cans beer
cold water
6 sachets instant dry yeast

In a large bowl, mix all the flour and salt. Bring the sugar, butter and beer to the boil. Remove from heat and add cold water – just enough to make the mixture lukewarm. Add the yeast and allow to ferment for 30 minutes. Pour the yeast mixture into the dry ingredients and mix to form a wet dough. Add more water if necessary. Allow to prove until double in size. Place in small clay flowerpots and allow to stand for 10 minutes. Bake at 180 °C for about 1 hour.

makes 36 mini-loaves

trout drambuie

Critchley Hackle Lodge, Dullstroom, Mpumalanga

4 whole rainbow trout
20 ml butter
juice of 1 lemon

drambuie sauce
65 ml butter
5 ml dried origanum
250 ml plain yoghurt
250 ml whipped cream
25 ml Drambuie
salt and freshly ground
   black pepper

pink mayonnaise
350 ml mayonnaise
100 ml tomato sauce
5 ml Worcestershire sauce

garnish
lemon twists
spring onion

Oven-grill the trout at 200 °C for 15 minutes basting occasionally with lemon butter. Remove the skin of the side facing up and baste with lemon butter. Set trout aside and keep warm.

For the Drambuie sauce, combine butter, origanum, yoghurt, whipped cream, Drambuie, salt and pepper. Boil over low heat for 10 minutes.

For the pink mayonnaise, mix the ingredients, bring to the boil and remove from heat.

To serve, spoon 45–60 ml mayonnaise onto a fish plate. Place whole trout on top. Pour Drambuie sauce over the trout. Garnish with a lemon twist and spring onion.

serves 4

wine suggestion
Bouchard Finlayson Chardonnay

critchley's beer bread

trout drambuie

phyllo parcels of crab, spring onion and ginger with a sweet-and-sour pepper salsa

Highgrove House,
Mpumalanga

salsa

1 small red pepper
1 small yellow pepper
2 tomatoes
1 baby marrow
1 shallot
1 clove garlic
1 green chilli
30 ml sunflower oil
rind and juice of 1 lime
5 ml sesame oil
salt and freshly ground
   black pepper

crab parcels

1 piece fresh root ginger
375 g white crab meat
2 stalks lemon grass
8 spring onions
salt and cayenne pepper
5 ml soya sauce
15 ml chopped fresh
   coriander
90 g unsalted butter
8 sheets phyllo pastry,
   each 18 cm x 9 cm

For the salsa, roast and skin the peppers. Dice half of each pepper and keep the rest for use in salads. Skin tomatoes, cut in half, remove cores and seeds. Dice tomato flesh. Trim and dice baby marrow. Peel and chop shallot. Peel and crush garlic. Cut chilli in half, remove core and seeds, then chop finely.

Heat the sunflower oil in a small pan. Add shallot, garlic and chilli to taste. Fry until soft, but not brown. Add baby marrow and cook for a few seconds until it turns bright green. Remove from heat and add lime rind and juice and sesame oil. Season and leave for at least 1 hour for the flavours to infuse.

For the phyllo parcels, preheat the oven to 230 °C. Blanch the root ginger, slice thinly, then julienne. Thoroughly check the crab meat for pieces of shell. Trim the lemon grass and remove the outer leaves. Use the tender white part only, finely chopped. Trim and slice the spring onions.

Combine the crab, ginger, lemon grass and spring onions in a small bowl. Add the salt, pepper, soya sauce and coriander.

Melt the butter. Cut phyllo rectangles in half to make 16 squares. Brush each square with melted butter. Using 2 squares, place one over the other, giving a quarter turn to make 8 pointed stars. Keep unbuttered phyllo covered to prevent drying. Place a little of the crab mixture in the centre of each star. Collect up the sides and gather them, giving a little twist to make the shape of an old-fashioned money bag. Place the phyllo parcels on a baking sheet and brush with the remaining butter. Bake in a preheated oven for about 15 minutes until crisp and golden. Plate parcels on a bed of the warmed salsa.

serves 4

wine suggestion

Thelema Sauvignon Blanc

fillet of pork stuffed with prunes and cranberries

Highgrove House,
Mpumalanga

Trim the pork of skin and fat.

For the stuffing, fry shallots and garlic in butter until softened. Add prunes and cranberry sauce. Cook gently for a couple of minutes, add breadcrumbs, port and seasoning. The mixture should be the consistency of a stiff paste. Allow to rest.

For the sauce, fry shallots and garlic in butter, add flour and cook gently for a couple of minutes, then slowly add stock stirring all the while, to make a smooth sauce. Add rosemary, prunes, cranberry sauce and port, cooking slowly for about 15 minutes. Allow to rest.

For the pork, preheat the oven to 200 °C. Very carefully make a hole lengthways in the pork, big enough to put your finger through. Using a piping bag with a plain nozzle, force some stuffing into the hole. Place in an ovenproof dish, brush with butter and season. Cook in the oven for 20 minutes.

To serve, heat the sauce, strain and add cream. Heat again, but do not boil. Cut pork into slices and serve with sauce. Garnish with rosemary and cranberries.

serves 8

wine suggestion
Hamilton Russel Pinot Noir

175 g fillet of pork

stuffing
125 g shallots, finely chopped
2 cloves garlic, chopped
125 g butter
125 g prunes, pitted and chopped
75 g cranberry sauce
125 g wholemeal bread crumbs
port to taste
salt and pepper

sauce
125 g shallots
1 clove garlic, chopped
50 ml butter
100 ml cake flour
600 ml chicken stock
large sprig rosemary
125 g prunes
50 g cranberry sauce
50 ml port
125 ml double cream

garnish
sprigs of rosemary
whole cranberries

lemon roast chicken

Critchley Hackle Lodge, Dullstroom, Mpumalanga

1 large free-range chicken
800 g sweet potato, sliced
60 ml chopped fresh
   origanum
60 ml chopped fresh thyme
salt and freshly ground
   black pepper
3 lemons
100 ml olive oil

Preheat oven to 220 °C. Cut chicken into portions and remove extra skin. Place sweet potatoes and chicken in a pan. Season with herbs, salt and pepper. Slice lemons and place on chicken. Drizzle with olive oil. Roast for 45–60 minutes.

serves 6

wine suggestion
Bouchard Finlayson Chardonnay

cherry bumpers

Critchley Hackle Lodge, Dullstroom, Mpumalanga

450 g puff pastry
500 g cherries, stalked
   and stoned
75 g brown sugar
milk
castor sugar

Roll out the pastry to 5 mm thick. Cut out saucer-sized rounds. Cover one half of each round with cherries, leaving a border of 1 cm, and sprinkle with brown sugar. Dampen the border, fold over and press sides together. Brush with milk and sprinkle with castor sugar, then bake in a preheated oven at 220 °C for 20–25 minutes, until golden brown.

Makes 6–8

wine suggestion
Van Loveren Red Muscadel

lemon roast chicken

cherry bumpers

contributing restaurants

THE WEST COAST

Evita se Perron
Darling Station
(022) 492 2851

When Pieter-Dirk Uys and his alter-ego, the flamboyant and outrageous Evita, puts on a show each Friday, Saturday and Sunday, the *perron* – station platform – and bistro are crowded with theatregoers from as far afield as Cape Town, 50 km away, eager for a dose of his wicked wit and flagrant disdain for the Establishment.

The Slipway Waterfront Restaurant
The Harbour, Saldanha Bay

A large informal eaterie on the water's edge at Saldanha Bay, 90 minutes from Cape Town. Fresh mussels and oysters are a speciality, as is fresh line fish when available. The menu also offers vegetarian pastas and salads, and for confirmed carnivores, there are mouthwatering steaks and ribs.

The Old Palm
St Helena Bay
(022) 736 1704

Vissermans Kombuis
Paternoster
083 463 8181

Housed in a whitewashed cottage, typical of the region, this restaurant offers excellent steaks, and fresh seafood. The wine list features West Coast wines, and a selection from the Robertson district.

THE CAPE PENINSULA & WINELANDS

The Atlantic Grill at the Table Bay Hotel
Quay 6, Waterfront 8002
(021) 406 5000

A sumptuous venue of grand proportions, superb décor and exquisite classic cuisine. The Atlantic Grill serves à la carte breakfasts, lunches and dinners, with the emphasis on the finest local seafood and other produce. It has an open-face wine cellar stocked with 6 000 bottles of the best South African wines, and Champagne. For cigar smokers, there is a choice of fine cigars stored under optimum conditions.

Bosman's at Grand Roche Hotel
Plantasie Street, Paarl 7646
(021) 863 2727

Bosman's has won numerous awards for its cuisine and wine list. It remains the only establishment in Africa to have received the prestigious Relais Gourmand status. It was awarded the acclaimed Jeanette James Trophy by the Chaine des Rotisseurs for the best Chaine Restaurant during 1996.

Franschoek Country House
Main Road, Franschhoek
(021) 876 3386

Haute Cabrière Cellar Restaurant
Pass Road, Franschhoek 7690
(021) 876 3688

Haute Cabrière is situated high up on the Franschhoek Pass. Cellar-master Achim von Arnim's Pinot Noir vineyard produces *methode champenoise* and classic cultivar wines. The menu is designed to complement the wines, and includes much of the valley's own produce, particularly fresh salmon trout. Named one of the top 10 restaurants in the country.

Die Ou Pastorie
41 Lourens Street, Somerset West 7130
(021) 852 2120

Eleganty housed in a historic parsonage, this award-winning restaurant has been named one of the top 100 in South Africa. Although its approach is classic, the cuisine reflects the chef's innovative flavour combinations, using the freshest ingredients. The wine list has been the recipient of The Diners Club Award in 1996, 1997, 1998 and 1999. Breakfast, lunch and dinner are served daily. Light lunches are served on the terrace.

KAROO & NORTHERN CAPE

Andries Stockenström Guesthouse
100 Cradock Street, Graaff-Reinet
(049) 892 4575

Beautifully appointed in an 1819 building named for its earliest resident, Governor Andries Stockenström. The restaurant caters mainly for visitors to the guesthouse, so to be certain of a table, you'd best book a bed for the night. Voted winner of the best full-service guesthouse in South Africa, 1997–1999.

Bernhard se Taphuis
10 Baron Van Rheedestraat, Oudtshoorn 6626
(044) 272 3208

Country cuisine at its best, and fine wines of the region. Above the restaurant, the Ostrich Hunting Bar and adjoining balcony offer a convivial venue for stylish drinks and light meals.

The Victoria Room
Swartberg Country Lodge, Kerk Street, Prince Albert
(023) 541 1332

The Swartberg Country Lodge is a gracious Victorian-style hotel. The Victoria Room serves traditional South African and regional cuisine, deliciously prepared, using the very best Karoo lamb, as well as game such as ostrich and kudu. It also boasts an award-winning wine list.

GARDEN ROUTE, OVERBERG & EASTERN CAPE

The Burgundy Restaurant
cnr Marine Drive and Harbour Road, Hermanus
(028) 312 2800

Set in a low, whitewashed cottage – the oldest building in the village and a National Monument – the Burgundy serves dinners and al fresco lunches against a backdrop of one of the world's most famous whale-watching sites – Walker Bay. The restaurant is best known for its consistently stunning seafood.

The Cock House Guesthouse and Restaurant
10 Market Street, Grahamstown
(04636) 1287

Housed in a gracious 1826 National Monument with gleaming yellowwood floors, the Cock House is one of the Eastern Cape's best known hostelries.

Greyton Lodge
46 Main Street, Greyton
(028) 254 9876

Greyton Lodge, built in 1882, was once the village police station. Roast beef and Yorkshire pudding are great Sunday lunch favourites. Winner of five Diners Club awards for its wine list. The ceiling is a real curiosity – 15 000 wine corks are attached to it, reminding visitors of good times gone by.

La Loerie
57 Main Street, Knysna
(04438) 21616

La Loerie takes its name from the Knysna lourie, a bird endemic to the region. Although the owners describe their cuisine as unpretentious, the regulars will testify to an exotic slant that keeps them coming back for their favourite dishes.

The Marine Hotel
Marine Drive, Hermanus
(028) 313 1000

The Marine is a luxury hotel at the ocean's edge, overlooking the cliff path and Walker Bay. Mostly seafood, but pasta and salads are also on the menu.

The Med
Village Square, Main Street, Plettenberg Bay
(044) 533 3102

Here the dishes – meat, pasta, salads and especially seafoods – are simply prepared so that the diner can enjoy the true flavours. The wine list, which has achieved Diner's Club merit awards, includes estate wines, fortified wines, and brandies.

KWAZULU-NATAL

Granny Mouse's Country House
R103 Old Main Road, Balgowan
(033) 234 4071

Deep in the scenic Natal Midlands on a 25-ha estate, Granny Mouse Country House is a dream weekend get-away destination. Dinner is culinary heaven, with a sumptuous five-course table d'hôte spread and a menu that changes nightly. The fare is simply elegant, fresh and perfectly tuned with the seasons. The award-winning underground cellar houses a collection of fine estate wines, Ports and Champagnes.

Rainbow Terrace
Hilton Hotel Durban
12 Walnut Road, Durban 4001
(031) 336 8100

The informal Rainbow Terrace restaurant is a brasserie-style venue. A mouth-watering lunch and dinner buffet is available daily, featuring a large selection of appetizers, delectable salads, soup of the day, smoked fish and seafood platters, curries and a sumptuous carvery. The dessert selection is renowned.

The Sunday lunch buffet is designed to be enjoyed *en famille*, with an array of traditional specialities complementing the roast of the day.

The Royal Grill
267 Smith Street, Durban
(031) 304 0331

Thokozisa Mountain Café
PO Box 378, Winterton 3340
(036) 488 1273

Thokozisa Mountain Café offers its guests only the freshest and most natural ingredients on a hearty, varied menu. Its location is in one of the most beautiful parts of the Drakensberg, with panoramic views from Cathedral Peak all the way to Monk's Cowl. Visitors sit out-of-doors in fine weather, sheltered by a huge pagoda.

In winter, tables are set indoors beside a wood-burning stove. The Café is renowned for its coffee, home-baked cakes and traditional ginger beer. Bountiful salads are stuffed with fresh herbs from the permaculture gardens on the property, and home-made chutneys and relishes add zest to a fine selection of curries. The hand-made pastas are embellished with fresh mountain trout and delectable sauces, which include fresh cream, whole milk, free-range eggs and a variety of home-grown vegetables and herbs. The Café is open for breakfast, and throughout the day for full meals or snacks.

FREE STATE

Cranberry Cottage
37 Beeton Street, Ladybrand 9745
(051) 924 2290

Cranberry Cottage emphasises freshness, both in the simplicity of the décor and the wonderful variety of home-grown vegetables that appear on the table. The area is famous for cherries, asparagus, trout and duck and these are regulars on the menu. The cuisine is described as a melange of various styles – inspiration comes from what's available on that day, and on the humour of the chef.

Maluti Mountain Lodge
Clarens, Free State
(058) 256 1422

A cornucopia of arcadian pleasures awaits the traveller in the scenic Clarens area, on the border of the Golden Gate Highlands National Park in the eastern Free State: streams rich with trout, rolling hills, tree-studded valleys, and soaring sandstone cliffs.

The Highland Grill restaurant specialises in steak, duck, trout, oxtail, lamb and, in season, venison. The food is hearty and delicious, eschewing any notions of *nouvelle cuisine* or city diets. Winter in the mountains is cold, and heartwarming stews and thick, hot soups served in front of roaring log fires are *de rigueur*.

GAUTENG, NORTHERN PROVINCE & NORTH-WEST

Chagall's Restaurant
924 Park Street, Arcadia, Pretoria
(012) 342 1200

Chagall's was founded 11 years ago as an extension to the renowned Toulouse Restaurant, but has recently established its independence – and a strong culinary personality – in handsome premises in an old house in Park Street. The cuisine is distinguished by a playful overlay of modern trends on a firm foundation of classic French tradition. Chagall's chefs have always been

French, and each has brought his unique signature to the table. This one introduces an Oriental influence, another elevates pasta to an art form, yet another delights in shocking, with combinations of surprising ingredients that nevertheless rest pleasantly on the palate. The result is a menu that is always original, and which pays homage to Chagall's fine cellar that offers affordable *vins ordinaires* as well as some rare and noble vintages.

Guests may sit indoors or, on clear nights, dine under the stars on the intimate patio. The décor is a joyful mix of bright pastel mauve, lime and orange to set off the simple elegance of white table settings, and the informal and relaxed atmosphere is given context by the harmony of colour and form, which typifies the work of its namesake artist, Marc Chagall.

Gramadoelas Restaurant
Market Theatre Complex, Newtown
PO Box 17770, Hillbrow 2038
(011) 838 6960

Gramadoelas is a legend in Johannesburg. Established 34 years ago, it has consistently been a favourite destination for hungry celebrities from pop stars to princes, poets to politicians. Her Majesty Queen Elizabeth II had lunch here on her recent visit to South Africa, and the years have seen a stately procession of royal and loyal supporters, including Nelson Mandela, the Queen of Denmark, Hillary Clinton, Mrs John Major, Catherine Deneuve, Nadine Gordimer, Harry Belafonte, Stevie Wonder, David Bowie and his beautiful wife Iman.

A French food writer wrote: 'If you are foolish enough to want to eat outside France, and you happen to be in Johannesburg, try the Gramadoelas.' *Gramadoelas* is a Khoisan word meaning 'an African heaven' – and few who have enjoyed the fruits of this table, or the generous hospitality, could disagree.

Villa del Palazzo
Palace of the Lost City

The Villa del Palazzo, flagship restaurant of Sun City, is at the Palace of the Lost City, pivot of the giant resort 187 kilometres from Johannesburg. Approached from behind a waterfall in the Palace garden, the restaurant, surrounded by water, serves delectable Italian dishes, with the emphasis on seafood. Superbly grilled line fish, platters of a variety of seafoods delicately prepared, and the best of Italian cuisine are served in a grand setting by hospitable and knowledgable staff. The desserts are entirely divine and are variations on an Italian theme.

MPUMALANGA

Critchley Hackle Lodge
Pebing van Berkhout Street, Dullstroom 1110
(01325) 40145

Situated in the uplands of Mpumalanga, Critchley Hackle Lodge offers a delightful combination of trout-fishing, elegant country accommodation and fine cuisine. The focal point is, of course, the well-stocked trout lake, but there is plenty more to occupy the visitor in and around the lodge and its beautiful environs. The stone-built rooms are individually decorated and superbly appointed, each with a log-fire for the crisp winter months. Dullstroom is well situated for weekend get-aways, or a relaxing stopover just two hours' drive from Johannesburg International Airport en route the Kruger Park.

Highgrove House
between White River and Hazyview
PO Box 46, Kiepersol 1241
(013) 764 1844

Highgrove House, tucked away in a gloriously pastoral setting in the heart of Mpumalanga, combines unashamedly lavish accommodation with gourmet cuisine. Voted the best small luxury hotel in South Africa for three consecutive years, the dining room at Highgrove House has also been named one of the top 10 restaurants in South Africa. Each meal served in the candle-lit restaurant is accompanied by the country's finest wines and offers the best of South African hospitality and service.

The emphasis at the lodge is on privacy and luxury, combined with old-world charm and courtesy. Visitors are transported to another world at the entrance to the jacaranda-lined driveway, which leads to the gracious farmstead. The colonial-style building has been masterfully restored and converted for use as an elegant country lodge. Highgrove House is located just 25 minutes' drive from the Kruger Park, and is close to all the major attractions in this spectacularly scenic region.

index

general index